European Economic Legal Order After Brexit

Legacy, Regulation, and Policy

Enzo Cardi

European Economic Legal Order After Brexit

Legacy, Regulation, and Policy

Routledge
Taylor & Francis Group
LONDON AND NEW YORK

G. Giappichelli Editore

First published 2021
by Routledge
2 Park Square, Milton Park, Abingdon, Oxon OX14 4RN

and by Routledge
605 Third Avenue, New York, NY 10158

Routledge is an imprint of the Taylor & Francis Group, an informa business

British Library Cataloguing-in-Publication Data
A catalogue record for this book is available from the British Library

Library of Congress Cataloging-in-Publication Data
A catalogue record for this book has been requested

ISBN: 978-0-367-70138-3 (hbk-Routledge)
ISBN: 978-1-003-14475-5 (ebk-Routledge)
ISBN: 978-1-032-05540-4 (pbk -Routledge)
ISBN: 978-88-921-3672-4 (hbk-Giappichelli)

Typeset in Simoncini Garamond
by G. Giappichelli Editore, Turin, Italy

The manuscript has been subjected to a peer review process prior to publication.

CONTENTS

LIST OF ABBREVIATIONS

ACER – Agency for the Cooperation of Energy Regulators
BEREC – Body of European Regulators for Electronic Communications
BVerfG – *Bundesverfassungsgericht* (Federal Constitutional Court)
CETA – Canada Comprehensive Economic and Trade Agreement
CMA – Competition and Markets Authority
CJEU – Court of Justice of the European Union
EASA – European Union Aviation Safety Agency
EBA – European Banking Authority
ECB – European Central Bank
ECN – European Competition Network
EEA – European Economic Area
EEC – European Economic Community
EFTA – European Free Trade Association
EIOPA – European Insurance and Occupational Pensions Authority
ELA – Emergency Liquidity Assistance
EMS – European Monetary System
EMU – Economic and Monetary Union
EMS – European Monetary System
ERM – European Exchange Rate Mechanism
ESA – European Supervisory Authorities
ESCB – European System of Central Banks
ESFS – European System of Financial Supervision
ESM – European Stability Mechanism
ESMA – European Securities and Markets Authority
EURATOM – European Atomic Energy Community

FCA – Financial Conduct Authority
FSA – Financial Services Authority
FTA – Free Trade Agreement
GATS – General Agreement on Trade in Services
GATT – General Agreement on Tariffs and Trade
GPA – Government Procurement Agreement
IMF – International Monetary Fund
IEM – Internal Energy Market
LMU – Latin Monetary Union
MFF – Multiannual Financial Framework
MREL – Minimum Requirement for own funds and Eligible Liabilities
NCAs – National Competent Authorities
NCA – Nuclear Cooperation Agreement
NGEU – Next Generation EU
NAFTA – North American Free Trade Agreement
NRA – National Regulatory Authority
OIM – Office Internal Market
OMT – Outright Monetary Transactions
PEPP – Pandemic Emergency Purchase Programme
PRA – Prudential Regulation Authority
PSPP – Public Sector Purchase Programme
QE – Quantitative Easing
SGI – Services of General Interest
SRB – Single Resolution Board
SRF – Single Resolution Fund
SGP – Stability and Growth Pact
SMU – Scandinavian Monetary Union
SRM – Single Resolution Mechanism
SSM – Single Supervisory Mechanism
TCA – Trade and Cooperation Agreement
TEN – Trans-European Networks
TFUE – Treaty on the Functioning of the European Union
TSCG – Treaty on Stability, Coordination and Governance

TEU – Treaty on European Union
W&M – Ways and Means (monetary financing)
WTO – World Trade Organization

PREFACE

At the beginning of the third decade of the 21st century, the legal systems of the EU and the UK face challenges of epic proportions.

Never before have the two ***legal orders*** *been confronted with the simultaneous impact of a series of events:*

- *The effect of the "divorce" between the two regulatory systems caused by the UK's withdrawal from the EU legal order. The expiry of the transition period triggered the start of two separate legal systems* as of January 1, 2021.
- *The impact of the coronavirus shock on all European economies. The effect is a substantial change of political perspective in EU legal orders. It is being addressed with the "Temporary Framework" for state aid, the "Escape Clause" in the Stability and Growth Pact (SGP) and the "Next Generation European Union Recovery Fund" for the creation of new common assets.*

The dramatic relaunch of the debate on ***identity*** *issues throughout Europe, the EU institutions' response to the pandemic shock and the impact of this response on European monetary policy are all addressed in this book within the framework of a "Public Regulatory Law" text.*

The book questions the effect resulting from the ***legacy*** *(Part One) of an historical period in which the EU and the UK were part of a "single legal order", the impact on* ***market regulation*** *of the striking events of our time (Part Two), and the consequences on* ***policy*** *(monetary, fiscal and trade) of the current convulsive political and financial landscape (Part Three).*

Its "file rouge" is the idea – developed throughout the book – that ***terminology, concepts*** *and* ***models*** *originating from two historically different experiences, the Anglo-Saxon and the continental (with all the variety of the latter), have cross-fertilized each other. This forms the* *basis of the shared platform for the* ***Future Relationship****, the title given by the UK Parliament to the* ***Act*** *that on 30 December 2020 ratified the* ***Trade and Cooperation Agreement****, sealed by the EU and the UK on Christmas Eve 2020 and which entered into force on January 1, 2021.*

The regulatory system born out of this mutual fertilization is now a reservoir the Parties may rely on to feed their ***"separate markets"*** *and their "****distinct legal orders****": mutual debts due to mutual* ***intellectual influence*** *are the only real foundations for fair co-operation and competition, reaching far beyond the terms of a deal so long negotiated and shrouded in vague formulas open to conflicting interpretation.*

Enzo Cardi studied Law at the University of Rome "Sapienza" and Oxford University (St. John's College). He is currently Professor of Administrative Law and Regulation in Economics at "Roma Tre University".

January 1, 2021

ACKNOWLEDGMENTS

This book has been inspired by a unique period in which the EU and the UK were part of a "single legal order".

On a personal level, that period, by now an historical one, is marked by the temporal coincidence of having spent my post-graduate education at Oxford in the years following the "first" referendum on UK accession.

The extraordinary cultural milieu of St. John's College and the Oxford Faculty of Law suggested paths for exploring the contamination among cultural sources far beyond the specific law study field.

With some of my contemporary students at St. John's College – such as, and above all, the philosopher Richard Shusterman (currently Eminent Scholar in the Humanities at Florida Atlantic University) – the dialogue continued throughout this time.

Beyond a circle of personal acquaintances, I owe a specific debt of gratitude to Prof. Patrick Gèrard (Directeur de l'École National d'Amnistration, Strasbourg), Prof. Veronique A. Lafon-Vinais (Professor of Business Education at Hong Kong University of Science and Technology), Prof. Carolyn Kadas (Professor of Economics of Transition in Eastern Europe at University of Bologna) for suggestions deriving from different angles and perspectives.

For all the others from whom I have drawn suggestions or hints over time, without mentioning them all, my feelings can only be expressed in the following Shakespearean verse:

"I count myself in nothing else so happy / As in a soul remembering my good friends" [Richard II, Act 2, sc. 3].

Introduction
IDENTITY

"We are with Europe, but not of it.
We are linked, but not compromised.
We are interested and associated,
but not absorbed"
(W. CHURCHILL, 1930)

From a "Moral Idea" to an "Economic" Issue

The underlying concept of the above quoted famous words is obviously a reaffirmation of "identity".

In general constitutional terms, "identity" is a challenging word that bases its legitimacy on the popular vote.

*In political terms, identity politics is – in the words of Francis Fukuyama – a **"moral idea"** from which "we cannot get away":*

> *"It focuses on natural demand for recognition of our dignity [...] expressing the resentments that arise when such recognition is not forthcoming"* [F. FUKUYAMA (2019)].

A moral idea formed in the constitutional order that is far from being exclusive to the UK. Political theorists stress the need to not underestimate the deep implications of the notion itself of identity for national communities in contemporary times:

> *"Souvent tournées vers la défense d'identités anciennes menacées, nourries de protectionnisme et de nationalisme, elles font l'apologie des identités et des racines, ressenties comme des valeurs stables dans un monde précaire"* [J. ATTALI (2018)].

*At the extreme limit of its consequences lies the concept of **secession**, a term that refers to the territory of a state (as in the Scotland and Catalan* *claims) and which is obviously different from "withdrawal" from a supranational membership. However, the logic of* ***withdrawal*** *from the EU and secession from the territory of a state have one thing in common:*

> *"a failure of the rationalist project of sharing a polity out of rational choice, and the will of doing so".* [C. CLOSA (2017)]

This failure of the ***rationalist*** *project of* ***sharing a polity*** *was made explicit in the position paper published on 27 February 2020 by the UK government with a view to negotiating the new partnership with the EU following the Withdrawal Agreement:*

> *"at the end of the transition period provided for in that agreement, the UK will fully recover its economic and political independence" [****UK's Approach to negotiations****, sec. 2].*

A distinctive notion of identity emphasized by the prospective to "embark on an exciting new phase as an independent trading nation" (*as remarked in the subsequent* **UK Internal Market White Paper**, *July* 2020) *and finally proudly underlined in the Foreword by the UK Government to the* ***Trade and Cooperation Agreement:***

> *the "Agreement means that the UK will fully recover its national independence […] restoring national sovereignty"* [UK **TCA Summary**, *Foreword from the Prime Minister*, December 2020].

On a more general level,

> *"nationalism promises a source of identity and security: a return to full sovereignty will supposedly stem the global forces responsible for today's uneasiness "* [E. CAMPANELLA, M. DASSÙ (2019)].

The theme is not at all exclusive to the UK.

Also significant – along these lines – is the fact that all the ***popular votes*** *that have been held in EU Member States on Europe's issues since the early years of the new millennium have had a* ***negative outcome****. The popular votes have all had to do with central issues: monetary, constitutional, fiscal and eventually membership. Obviously a referendum (including the Brexit case) tends to be dominated by internal political issues, but in any case, the European* ***democratic deficit*** *can* *be seen above all in the fact that, when they have had the opportunity, European countries have repeatedly rejected integration policies.*

The list begins with the Danish referendum on Economic and Monetary Union (EMU) in September 2000 with a negative result for EMU membership. Previously Denmark had also rejected the Maastricht Treaty; then approved it when it was granted the right, through a special Protocol, to not join the single currency. Subsequently, Sweden also voted in September 2003 to not join EMU.

The worst came with the "Constitution for Europe" signed (as it had already been for the 1957 Treaty) in Rome in October 2004 and rejected without hope of repackaging by referendum in France and the Netherlands in May and June 2005.

Ireland voted against the Lisbon Treaty in 2007. In 2015 the Greek electorate voted to reject the conditions imposed by the bailout programme.

In other cases, such as the treaty establishing the European Stability Mechanism (ESM) designed to rescue Eurozone Member States in financial difficulty (and relaunched in the current pandemic crisis for health security interventions) the choice to establish the mechanism through an international agreement instead of amending the EU treaties was due to the fact that the treaty amendments "would have required politically difficult referenda in a range of member states" [D. HOWARTH, L. QUAGLIA, in C.J. BICKERTON, D. HODSON, U. PUETTER (2015)].

All the referenda results can lead to the "obvious conclusion" that "the public opinion which governs a country is the opinion of the sovereign, whether the sovereign be a monarch […] or the mass of the people" [A.V. DICEY(1917)].

In all cases ***identity*** *has played a central role.*

On the contrary, and perhaps as a paradox, stand the only two plebiscites held in the United Kingdom before 2016. One was held in 2011 on changing the voting system for members of parliament, and the electorate voted in favour; the other was held in 1975 on membership in the (then) European Community and two thirds of the electorate voted to stay. An impressive difference was the fact that in 1975 "support in England was higher than in any other part of the United Kingdom" [B. SIMMS (2013)]: in 2016 England made the difference in favour of withdrawal.

The Quest for Identity

The "constitutional order" of the EU is based on an essential principle: *"the primacy"* of EU law *"in areas where legislative power had been conferred by Member States to their common institutions"* [G. AMATO, in J. BELL, C. KILPATRICK (2006)]. The *primacy* of EU law together with *direct effect* and *mutual recognition* are the **constitutional pillars** of the European legal system.

At the same time, the existence of reserved areas of state sovereignty is preserved in the treaties with particular reference to the ***national identities*** of states (Article 4 (2) TEU).

Any legal reference to national identity can be widely controversial as to its actual meaning. As historians point out

> *"There is a kind of circularity: the nation state represents national interests effectively because its very existence defines those interests"* [J. BLACK (2019)].

In any case, since these interests belong to the *political process* – and the dynamics of interests in the EU context demonstrate the *lack* of a *living concept* of ***European polity*** – they are used by nation states: at least at present it is far from clear that a European political community can successfully carry out the same function.

Indeed, national identity has always been an issue in the European integration project:

> *"The search for a common European identity has been hugely problematic throughout the history of the EU. It is widely interpreted as a kind of nation-building that both conflicts with and challenges the interests of nation-states"* [M. SHACKLETON, in B. MARTILL, U. STAIGER (2018)].

As for the UK, it is not surprising that the debate on the issue of *"national primacy"* preceded the referendum debate. National primacy had already been reinforced by the role of parliamentary procedures for the enactment of EU rules (through the Westminster *European Select Security Committee*) acting – at least for primary legislation – *"as a form of substitute Sovereignty"* [D.J. GALLIGAN (2014)] on the basis of *"parliamentary accountability for EU affairs"* [A. CYGAN, in A.J. CORNELL, M. GOLDONI (2017)].

In the British legal and constitutional experience, the point was subject to *acrobatic theories* in order to give priority to the economic benefits over the constitutional implications of EU membership:

> *"Instead of conceiving European Law as an "autonomous" legal order that directly applied within the United Kingdom* [...] *the official view continued to insist that absolute – British – supremacy remains untouched. For instead of locating the supremacy of (earlier) European law over (later) Westminster legislation in the European legal order, the British view came to locate it in the (English) common law"* preserving *"the supremacy of British over European law"* [R. SCHÜTZE, in R. SCHÜTZE, S. TIERNEY (2018)].

In fact, the doctrine of parliamentary sovereignty throughout the period of UK membership has been an endless refrain, including – as already mentioned – the acrobatic effort to support the assumption that EU law primacy was not in conflict with Dicey's classical doctrine: the primacy of EU law is

> *"a constitutional development which fundamentally operates so as to preserve the sovereignty of Parliament"* because it *"is a reconfiguration, and not a repudiation, of the idea of legally unlimited legislative authority"* [M. GORDON (2015)].

Again, the **European Union (Withdrawal) Act 2020** approved by the British Parliament on 23 January 2020 considered it necessary or in any case useful to reiterate – precisely at the end of EU membership – the principle that the UK Parliament is sovereign even during the (now expired) transition period, *"notwithstanding directly applicable or directly effective EU law continuing to be recognized and available in domestic law"* (sec. 38 (2)(a)).

Significantly, the section ends with a clear emphasis:

> *"Accordingly, nothing in this Act derogates from the sovereignty of the Parliament of the United Kingdom".*

An enphasy on identity reinforced, if possible, by the plural concept of "nation" as in the **White Paper 2020** on **Internal Market** (July 2020) that outlines plans for a new UK internal market among the "*four constituent nations*" (one of which, Northern Ireland, continues to comply with EU customs rules), enabling the "*seamless* *functioning*" of commerce among the four nations (embraced in the "*unitary state*" concept).

A "Judicial secession": the Case of the German Constitutional Court

In any case, the apparent record of institutionalized *exceptionalism* that accompanied the British constitutional commitment to EU obligations is by no means exclusive. Its approach to the *constitutional issue* of sovereign and national identity is widely shared by several Member States.

Without using the same wording, but using the same concepts, several national constitutional courts have spoken out, saying that there must be limits to European integration, limits that are imposed by national constitutions as certain areas are too essential for the *sovereignty* or *identity* of the state.

Specific *national constitutional requirements* can filter out the application of European public law when – as a German constitutionalist stated –

> "*national constitutional courts or supreme courts with constitutional jurisdiction can review treaties as to their compatibility with the national constitution*" [D. GRIMM (2016)].

It is sufficient to recall the case law of the German Constitutional Court of Justice (*Bundesverfassungsgericht*, *BVerfG*), over the last three decades, starting with a very clear judgment on the limits of integration on the Maastricht decision [*BVerfG*, 2 BvR 2134/92 (1993)].

The Court stated that Germany's ***constitutional identity*** requires a legitimate democratic government and therefore democratic representation of the type found at state level is necessary to regulate or legitimately govern areas of EU competence. The Court concluded that within the *current constitutional framework* there would always be certain areas of competence that should remain within the sphere of national democracy, giving a constitutional basis to the notion of "*multi-level structure*" [E. SCHMIDT AßMANN (2015)].

A further transfer of competences would go against the constitutional identity of Germany, or, rather, would imply the risk of diluting the state into a *less democratic supranational entity*. Neither the German Constitution nor the Court would allow this:

> *"while the BVerfG has never prevented the ratification of an EU treaty so far, its case law has restricted the room of negotiation for the German government on EU affairs. In its Lissabon Urteil, BVerfG 123, 267 (2009), the BVerfG has identified a core set of competences which belong to the heart of state sovereignty and which cannot be transferred to the EU"* [F. FABBRINI (2017)].

Other decisions taken over the years concern the legal limits of the European Central Bank (ECB) [*BVerfG*, 2 BvR 1390/12 (2012)] or the ECB's policies on stabilization of the euro, as was the case for *outright monetary transactions (OMT)* [*BVerfG*, 2 BvR 2728/13 (2016)] and for *quantitative easing* [*BVerfG*, 2 BvR 859/15 (2017)]. In light of the above rulings, the independence of the ECB

> *"est vue comme une exception au principe de démocratie, exception devant naturellement être justifiée par une raison particulièrement forte. La Cour constitutionnelle fédérale allemande (Bundesverfassungsgericht) justifie cette exception par l'objectif de stabilité monétaire"* [J.H. KLEMENT, in G. KALFLECHE, T. PERROUD, M. RUFFERT (2018)].

The same pattern has been followed in the latest judgment [*BVerfG*, 2 BvR 859/15 (2020)] in which the ECB was asked to justify the legal grounds for the bond purchase programmes pursued by the ECB in recent years. The ruling is framed in reasoning focused on criticism of a previous CJEU ruling on the issue [Judgment of 11 December 2018, *Weiss and Others*, C-493/17, EU:C:2018:1000]. The criticism seems to allow a national constitutional court – such as the *Bundesverfassungsgericht* – to rule on the consistency of the CJEU judicial reasoning and this on the assumption that the CJEU judgment in this specific case is "*untenable from a methodological perspective*". On the basis of this assumption, a court of a Member State argues that:

> *"the interpretation of the principle of proportionality undertaken by the CJEU, and the determination of the ESCB's mandate based thereon, exceed the judicial mandate conferred upon the CJEU"* [*BVerfG*, 2 BvR 859/15 (2020)].

Therefore, a national constitutional court may claim the constitutional **authority** to review a CJEU decision (belonging to a supranational legal order and as such independent from Member States' national legal orders), and then apodictically conclude on the point that:

> *"In light of the aforementioned considerations, the Federal Constitutional Court is not bound by the CJEU's decision but must conduct its own review to determine whether the Eurosystem's decisions* [...] *remain within the competences conferred upon it under EU primary law"* [*Ibid.*].

These words, which expressly reject the primacy of EU law and the primacy of the CJEU as regards its interpretation, appeared to external observers as *"an act of judicial secession"*. This is particularly significant given the parameters of seizure of power and political influence of the country to which the BVerfG belongs:

> *"Divergences between courts of the member states as to the validity of such acts would indeed be liable to place in jeopardy the unity of the EU legal order"* [M. Wolf, *German court decides to take back control with ECB ruling*, *Financial Times*, 12 May 2020].

It is clear that any significant step towards *further economic* and *fiscal integration* will be closely *monitored* by the BVerfG in the future, resulting in an *ultra vires* challenge (as an allegation that supranational institutions have gone beyond the powers granted by the treaties). A perspective in which future amendments to the EU treaties – or new interpretations of them – could be considered capable of influencing the "*reserved domains*" is identified by the BVerfG.

With regard to the relationship between the BVerfG and the *Court of Justice European Union* (CJEU), the last judgment confirms – as stated by German lawyers – that

> *"the Constitutional Court considers the relationship between the two courts as a form of 'cooperation', although it is quite unclear what this means exactly. In practice, the Constitutional Court therefore refrains from a review of Community acts but still keeps its review powers as a kind of Damocles-sword in reserve, thereby forcing the European*

> *Court of Justice to take the views of the Constitutional Court of Justice into account"* [W. HEUN (2011)].

The Case for "reserved constitutional domains"

In other Member States the constitutional courts are equally attentive to these developments, referring – albeit in more nuanced terms – to similar **reserved domains**. Some of these courts base their reasoning on the need for explicit democratic legitimacy, while others just argue that certain areas are part of the core of state sovereignty.

The signing of international treaties is a devaluation of sovereignty, to which the constitutionalism of Member States reacts in various ways.

It suffices to mention the case of Denmark (the country that after the UK's withdrawal holds the record for the highest number of explicit opt-out agreements). The national identity provision is used here to justify a form of derogation from the "indivisibility" totem of the four freedoms.

One example of non-compliance with the principle of full movement and non-discrimination is the legal limit on the purchase of a second home by nationals of other Member States.

> *"In particular, this allows for 'protection' from the Treaty provisions on free movement of capital and services, which in principle would otherwise have the effect of ensuring that EU nationals can buy property in other Member States"*[U. NEERGARD, in A. BAKARDJIEVA ENGELBREKT, X. GROUSSOT (2019)].

This approach, legitimated by a special bilateral EU-Denmark protocol, allows the Danish Supreme Court to reinvigorate a kind of **judicial activism** by explicitly choosing to reject parts of EU law, *"thus undermining a cornerstone of the EU acquis by failing to apply the principle of the supremacy of EU law"* [*Ibid*].

The above succinct picture gives an idea of the **fragmentation of the institutional order** of the European Union, depicted by German scholars as one of the *"major crises of political order in European history"* [J. NEYER, in A. BAKARDJIEVA ENGELBREKT*et al.* (2019)].

Asymmetries at national level are the result – or the consequence – of constitutional constraints due to the fact that:

> *"EU decision-making is limited by the very nature of the constituent Treaties. National constitutions constrain political choice. It is inherent in their very nature"* [P. CRAIG, in A. BAKARDJIEVA ENGELBREKT *et al.* (2019)].

The Quest for an Overarching Polity

The UK withdrawal represents the first *reduction in the size* of the EU's external institutional borders. The oft mentioned case of Greenland's withdrawal in 1985 is not significant, as Greenland was not a Member State but a territory within the state of Denmark.

In political terms, Europe is currently defined by the **borders** of the European Union. The political borders remain uncertain depending on future accessions, since Europe *"est une notion géographique sans frontières avec l'Asie et une notion historique aux frontières changeantes"* [E. MORIN (1987)].

Going back in history, as is well known, the theme of reconnecting **national identities** with an **overarching polity** has been a recurring one. The origins of this theme can be traced back to the Carolingian empires which emerged in the 9th century, several centuries after the collapse of the Roman Empire. A recurring theme throughout the centuries recalls the *Landfrieden* of the Holy Roman Empire, as well as the *Universitas Christianorum,* which constituted the *"chief model"* [B. HEUSER (2019)] of a global political system on the continent. Instead

> *"the political and historical use of the term Europe and the use of European as a noun/adjective began to circulate and actually gained a foothold at a time that coincided with the period between the Renaissance and the Enlightenment"* [G. GALASSO, in G. AMATO, E. MOAVERO-MILANESI, G. PASQUINO, L. REICHLIN (2019)].

On the English side, the quest for an "overarching polity" has followed a totally different path, pursuing other meanings of the notion. Throughout the 19th century, English statesmen had a clear idea that sovereignty was not at all antithetical to what Pitt the Youngest called a sort of *"public law of Europe"*.The concept was reinforced by the conviction

> *"that the tide of events in Europe was heading inexorably towards nationalist and constitutionalist modernity along English lines"* [B. SIMMS (2016)].

The events of mid-century Italian unification in 1860-61 strongly influenced English statesmen, suggesting the hope that the British example would inspire new and old European states to introduce constitutionalism.

Sovereignty, *liberalism* and *constitutionalism* were closely interconnected in the political sense of the *public law of Europe*: a concept stemming from

> *"two themes which were to remain a constant in English, and later British, strategic debate: fear of the domination of the continent by a single power, and England's role as a balancer"* [*Ibid*].

The coexistence of national identity and overarching polity (the "public law of Europe") was therefore – at least theoretically – well rooted in the ideas of liberalism and constitutionalism emerging in the 19th century.

In this sense, recalling a *"common heritage"* and *"the formative influence on constitutional thought"*, it can be stated that:

> *"Among the approaches that contribute to contemporary ideas, the British tradition merits a special place for the constitutional legacy it has left"* [D.J. GALLIGAN (2014)].

Sectorial Constitutionalism

In current times, the relationship between **European constitutionalism** and the **legal orders** of the Member States is made up of complementarity but also conflict.

Issues of "national identity" are largely absorbed by **constitutional pluralism.** In the current era of "post-national law", conflicts of authority are inevitable.

> *"National law adheres to the territorial principle of authority and claims universal jurisdiction in its territory. By contrast, transnational law's claim of authority is substantially or functionally defined and limited"* [K. TUORI, in A. BAKARDJIEVA ENGELBREKT *et al.* (2019)].

While the above definition underlines the breadth of any constitutional theory of the *Staatenverbund* or the federal union, it also raises the issue of the intellectual foundations of the *Verfassungsbund,* e.g. *complementarity* between *legal orders* and *post-national law*.

The dialectic between institutional **identity** and **supranationality** is clearly reflected in the functioning of the EU institutions.

Tension has always existed between the *community principle* and *intergovernmentalism*. The *community principle* is that the Commission takes initiatives and the Member States, through the EU Council, composed of representatives of Member State governments, shall approve or disapprove proposals. *Intergovernmentalism*, on the other hand, relies on governments to take and negotiate initiatives. Recent years have witnessed a shift to intergovernmentalism, often overwhelmed by the dominant role of the two largest member countries.

Ultimately the search for national identity has led to a "plural form of differentiation" that has given rise to different **sectorial legal orders**, although none of these (defence, justice, foreign affairs, social welfare) have the "institutional" richness and completeness of the European Monetary Union (EMU) as an adequate and autonomous legal order based on the single currency.

Thus, *national identity* has nurtured all the various forms of closer and more rigorous *intergovernmental cooperation*, i.e. all powers remain in the hands of national officials and any cooperation often has to be agreed unanimously rather than by the majority of all participants.

Several *enhanced cooperation* clauses and *derogations* have played an appropriate role in *"alleviating tensions"* for a *"troubled membership"* (non-exclusive of the UK) [C. CLOSA (2017)].

All these clauses aim to achieve European ***governance without government***, a *networked, non-hierarchical structure*. Rather than concepts of sovereignty or representation, this form of EU governance is based on procedures of *negotiation*, *bargaining*, *sector agreements*, *and joint decisions*:

> *"it is hard to point, in these instances, to any measure of political accountability, of someone paying a political price, as would be the case in national politics"* [J.H.H. WEILER, in C. CLOSA (2017)].

Towards Distinct Legal Orders

Article 50 of the *Treaty on the European Union* (TEU), on withdrawal from the EU, is from this point of view the starting point for a shift from the EU post-national legal order to the EU-UK **distinct legal orders**.

The withdrawal provision was introduced into the EU legal system only by the Lisbon Treaty. It is reported that:

> *"In fact, according to Giuliano Amato, the main drafter of Article 50 TEU, this clause was never actually meant to be used"* [F. FABBRINI (2017)].

The silence of the previous treaties created an interpretative void on the exit option:

> *"Doctrinally, exit options remained contentious but the 1975 UK referendum on withdrawal from the Communities proved, pragmatically, the existence of the right to withdraw. No one contested the British government's assumed right to withdraw"* [C. CLOSA (2017)].

After this episode, no other state claimed the right. But it was the German Constitutional Court, in its above-mentioned ruling on the Maastricht Treaty, that constructed the ***right of withdrawal*** as an essential guarantee of national sovereignty.

It is therefore significant that in the preparatory works for the *Convention of the Future of Europe* (2002-2003) for the (subsequently aborted) *Constitution for Europe*, which laid down a first legal framework to the (then) Article 50, the British representative defended a strictly unilateral provision of withdrawal to be effective. The final text instead introduced both the negotiation period – conducted for the EU by the Commission "*in the light of guidelines provided by the European Council*" – and the provision for the transition period, creating a kind of limbo membership in which withdrawing states are still bound by EU legislation and the principle of "*sincere cooperation*" (Article 4 (3) TEU). This transition period, provided for in the article, is what the parties (the EU and UK) experienced after withdrawal (31 January 2020) for the remainder of the 2020.

The *EU (Withdrawal Agreement) Act* (EUWA 2020): the Applicable Law

The choice of withdrawal also requires legislation to complete the process.

From a legislative point of view, a crucial issue concerns the *status* of *EU law* after withdrawal.

On the UK side, the internal legislative process began with the presentation to Parliament of a bill, initially known – on the basis of iconoclastic furore aimed at making a **bonfire** of EU legislation – as the **Great Repeal** Bill.

The legislation was passed by the British Parliament as **The European Union (Withdrawal) Act 2018** [**EUWA**]. Entering into force on Exit Day (31 January 2020), the general aim was to regain "*control of our laws*" on the one hand and give *"as much certainty as possible"* on the other.

The need to legislate stems from the significant circumstance that the effects of accession were enshrined in the *European Communities Act* 1972 (ECA), a statute which made EU law internally effective in the UK legal system. Consequently, the legal effects of withdrawal required an act that encompasses both legal effects: *repeal* and *retention*.

The *European Union (Withdrawal) Act 2018* was partly amended by the **European Union (Withdrawal) Act 2020** which introduced provisions for the *"implementation period"*, but kept the previous act in force (the abbreviation [EUWA] therefore refers to the two acts as a single text).

The EUWA is based on three main elements:

– First, the abrogation of the European Communities Act (ECA) 1972: *"the European Communities Act 1972 is repealed on exit day"*(Sec. 1), while *"it continues to have effect into domestic law"* during the *implementation period* as the UK *"is to be treated as if it were a member of the EU during the implementation"* (sec. 2-3)

- Second, preserving the EU law in force on exit day (**retained law**). Parliament (and, where appropriate, the devolved legislators) will then be able to decide which elements of that law to retain, amend or override.
- Third, retained law will concern both:

- **EU-derived domestic legislation** (sec. 2 (1B))

"(I) EU-derived domestic legislation, as it has effect in domestic law immediately before exit day, continues to have effect in domestic law on and after exit day";

- **Direct EU legislation** (sec. 3 (1))

"Direct EU legislation, so far as operative immediately before exit day, forms part of domestic law on and after exit day".

The legislative wording used to establish the retaining effect is "**saving**" for EU "derived domestic legislation" and "**incorporating**" for "direct EU legislation".

The general approach is to ensure **continuity** in the application of rules already in force until they are repealed or amended by the legislative or devolved authorities.

It is curious – and apparently a paradox – that the "reluctant" UK has been the most consistent **transposer** of EU legislation during its membership. In the sensitive area of public procurement, for example, the UK was ready to transpose EU legislation through the *Public Contracts Regulations 2015* using the "copy out" technique, e.g. without substantive additional requirements to the original EU regulation. This contrasts with Germany, France, Italy and Spain – to mention the main Member States – which all recur to specific statutes or "codification texts" for more detailed additional regulations – the so-called "gold plating" technique – with dysfunctional results.

EUWA 2020: the Interpretation of the "acquis communautaire"

The *EUWA* is a significant text on the ***sources of law*** of the **new distinct UK legal order** and, as such, a text that concerns *interpretation.*

Some guiding principles are expressly set out:

> *"the principle of the supremacy of EU law does not apply to any enactment or rule of law passed or made on or after exit day"* (sec. 5 (1)); *"Accordingly, the principle of the supremacy of EU law continues to apply on or after exit day so far as relevant to the interpretation, disapplication or quashing of any enactment or rule of law passed or made before exit day"* (sec. 5(2)).

Clearly, "legal certainty" and "continuity" are the main reasons why ***EUWA*** must ensure the application and interpretation of EU rules as the domestic source of law.

The official position on the *"acquis communautaire"* was already expressed in the months following the referendum day:

> *"Our proposal to shift the 'acquis' – the body of EU law – into UK law at the point of exit is designed to make the process as smooth as possible. At the point of exit, the same rules and laws will apply, and it will then be for this Parliament to determine changes in the country's interest"* [Gov. UK, 17 January 2017].

The aim was to overcome – as far as possible – the uncertainties that could hinder the exit process by *"providing certainty and clarity"*, an approach that

> *"will preserve the rights and obligations that already exist in the UK under EU law and provide a secure basis for future changes to our domestic law. This allows businesses to continue trading in the knowledge that the rules will not change significantly overnight and provides fairness to individuals whose rights and obligations will not be subject to sudden change"* [Gov. UK, 15 May 2017].

Consequently, according to the ***EUWA***, existing EU law transposed (as *"EU derived domestic legislation"*) or directly entered into the domestic legal system of the United Kingdom (*direct-EU Legislation*) is *"subject to further domestic legislation that overrides it"* (sec. 36).

In the "opening statement" at the second reading of the then "repeal bill", the concepts – later formalized by parliamentary approval – were clearly stated:

> *"Just as important as the text of EU law is the interpretation of that law. For that reason, the Bill ensures that any question as to the mean-*

> *ing of retained EU law is to be decided in the UK courts in accordance with the CJEU's case law and retained general principles of EU law as they stood on exit day.*
> *This approach maximizes stability by ensuring that the meaning of the law does not change overnight, and only the Supreme Court and the High Court of Justiciary in Scotland will be able to depart from retained EU case law.*
> *They will do so on the same basis that they depart from their own case law. Any other approach would either actively cause uncertainty, or fossilize CJEU case law forever".*

The "Great Repeal" – a *"nomenclature singularly inappropriate for a measure that repealed little, and served primarily to convert the EU legal acquis into UK law"* [P. CRAIG, in F. FABBRINI, ed., (2020)] - is in fact – more than an **abrogation** – a process of **conversion** from a previous supranational legal system to a national system, and as a result the *acquis* remains valid in terms of *interpretation* of "derived" or "direct" EU legislation.

EUWA 2020: the Applicable Jurisdiction

The relevant principles on the jurisdiction of the CJEU are also expressed in the Withdrawal Agreement (hereinafter **Withdrawal Agreement** or the **Agreement**) signed on 17 October 2019 between the UK and the remaining 27 EU Member States. The Agreement ruled on *"pending cases" in any proceedings brought by or against the UK before the end of the transition period"* (Article 86), expired on 31 December 2020.

The **Withdrawal Agreement** stated that:

> *"judgments and orders of the Court of Justice of the European Union handed down before the end of the transition period* [...] *shall have binding force in their entirety on and in the United Kingdom"* [Article 89].

Consistently, the **EUWA** confirmed that

> *"provisions of Union law applied by the Agreement must be interpreted by UK courts in accordance with the decisions of the CJEU given before the end of the implementation period (Article 4 (4))",*

The parties of the Agreement shared similar principles for ongoing *"administrative procedures"* handled by EU institutions, bodies, offices and agencies *"initiated before the end of the transition period"* (Article 92).

Instead, as regards CJEU rulings subsequent to the implementation period (i.e. from January 1, 2021), *"the United Kingdom's judicial and administrative authorities"* may only observe

> *"due regard to relevant case law of the Court of Justice of the European Union handed down after the end of the transition period"* [EUWA, sec. 5].

The **legal position** presented to Parliament by the Attorney General (2018) during the legislative process clarified the point concerning **due regard.** The language of "due regard" indicates that

> *"Future decisions of the CJEU will not bind our courts, but our courts will have discretion to have regard to such decisions if they consider it relevant and appropriate to do so – in just the same way that our courts might at the moment refer to cases in other common law jurisdictions, such as Australia or Canada".*

By contrast, the general principles are that

> *"A court or tribunal is not bound by any principles laid down, or any decisions made, on or after exit day by the European Court, and cannot refer any matter to the European Court on or after exit day"* [EUWA, sec. 6 (1)].

Nevertheless, these principles adopted by the CJEU after exit day may be taken into account by a British court: *"so far as it is relevant to any matter before the court or tribunal"* (sec. 6 (2)) or referring to *"the validity, meaning or effect of any retained EU law is to be decided, so far as that law is unmodified"* (sec. 6 (3)).

Therefore, while in general terms the Supreme Court and the High Court will not be *"bound by any retained EU case law"* (sec. 6 (4)), CJEU "jurisprudence" will maintain some relevance for the UK Courts.

As has been noted,

> *"UK courts have caused fewer difficulties for the EU legal order than those from many other Member States"* [P. CRAIG (2015)].

This is a confirmation of the cross-fertilization between the EU and UK legal orders (often highlighted in the following chapters) according to which *"the UK is in general open as a legal system to external influence, a ready importer of ideas as well as an exporter"* [*Ibid*].

Finally, as confirmed in the following section of the ***EUWA***, courts may decide to depart from CJEU rulings when there is room to depart from a precedent:

> *"In deciding whether to depart from any retained EU case law, the Supreme Court or the High Court of Justiciary must apply the same test as it would apply in deciding whether to depart from its own case law"* [sec. 6 (5)].

The wording ("*apply the same test*") is a fundamental principle as it stems from the peculiarity of the *"English doctrine of precedent"*.

The coercive nature of the principle allows for a degree of flexibility to adapt the legal system to changing needs, according to the maxim of ancient Roman and Canon Law *"cessante ratione legis, cessat ipsa lex"* [R. CROSS (1977)].

EUWA 2020: the "retained" EU Law

On the basis of the above framework, according to **EUWA** provisions, from 1 January 2021, the "retained" legislation can only be amended by a primary act of Parliament or any other subordinate primary legislation *"so far as it is made under a power which permits such a modification"* (sec. 7 (2) (a)).

In the context of a comprehensive discipline on the **sources of law**, particular attention is given to **secondary legislation**, adopted by regulation to address specific situations such as:

> *a) "any failure of retained EU law to operate effectively, or*
> *b) any other deficiency in retained EU law"* (sec.8 (1)).

The wording recalls a long debate on the variable limits of delegated legislation,

> *"merely allowing updating of the original Act but some provisions giving very wide powers to change the substance of policy without limit"* [G. GANZ, in P. LEYLAND, T. WOODS (1997)].

Although limited in terms of competence for the above cases, the **EUWA** states that the secondary regulation takes on the status of primary source in this context:

> *"Regulations under subsection (1) may make any provision that could be made by an Act of Parliament"* (sec. 8 (5)).

The *transitional function* of this form of *delegated legislation* is confirmed by a period of two years beginning on exit day, after which the regulatory power expires. It is an example of what administrative classics theorists used to qualify as *"contingent legislation"* [C.T. CARR (1941)]. To quote another classic:

> *"the Government of England has not possessed since 1689 any general power of issuing decrees (règlements in the sense of continental law) in execution of legislation. Consequently, powers of issuing regulations and orders are given separately in relation to each function of government"* [I. JENNINGS (1959)].

The process is formally under parliamentary control, but *"naturally the scrutiny of delegated legislation is not Parliament's highest priority"* [A. TUCKER, in A. HORNE, A. LESUER (2018)]:*"and so the detailed scrutiny that accompanies the passage of a Bill through Parliament is absent"* [P. HARDY, in A. HORNE *et al.* (2018)].

The *Withdrawal Agreement*: Private/ Public Reading

The **EUWA** is the *unilateral* discipline of the effects of the ***new identity status***. The **Withdrawal Agreement** is instead the appropriate *bilateral* act legitimizing the "**quest**" for identity. From the perspective of the new distinct legal orders, the latter is the *original source* of the *diverging process* that creates the *new legal orders*.

As the ***Agreement*** is an international act giving rise to new distinct legal orders, the relevant issue was "who" is the interpreter in the implementation of the Agreement and "how" to resolve the dispute arising from its application.

The *"Institutional Provisions"* set out in the ***Agreement*** – for the transition period only –provided a binary solution.

On the one hand, as regards "who" is the *interpreter*, the ***Agreement*** established a Joint Committee composed of representatives of the Union and the UK and co-chaired by both (Article 164 (1)).

As regards the **settlement of disputes**, reference is made to *"cooperation and consultations"* (Article 167), that implies good faith and best effort as contractual obligations. If *"no mutually agreed solution has been reached"* a party as such *"may request the establishment of an arbitration panel"* with the other party before the *International Bureau of the Permanent Court of Arbitration* (Article 170). In this respect, the ***Agreement*** regulated in detail: the *establishment* of the *arbitration panel*, the *rules of procedure*, the *timeframe* of the procedure before the arbitration panel, *compliance* and a reasonable period of time for compliance, *remedies* in case of non-compliance (including private forms of compensation for damage, i.e. *"a lump sum or penalty payment to be paid to the complainant"*), and the binding nature of arbitration decisions (which are decided by majority vote, although there are no provisions providing for the publication of the arbitration panel opinions).

The general pattern is that of a relationship based on a ***contract***. Albeit within the limited scope of its implementation, the ***Withdrawal Agreement*** has turned out to be an agreement signed under the rules of the **international private legal order**.

The "private law nature" of the ***Agreement*** has been made even clearer from a potential dispute through the formal notification by the EU Commission to the UK Government against plans to breach the ***Agreement***. The **EU's Letter** (1 October 2020) was – in its intentions – the first step in the formal "*infringement proceeding*". It was due to an alleged breach of "*good faith*" by the UK Government, which submitted a bill (the **Internal Market Bill**) containing provisions that would unilaterally override the ***Agreement*** in some limited (but politically sensitive) parts (the Northern Ireland Protocol), through clauses narrowing the notification requirement to the EU on subsidy decisions. The contested clauses were subsequently dropped, so that the infringment proceding was halted.

The dispute settlement is a perspective that the **UK's Approach to**

negotiations (the position paper published by the UK Government on 27 February 2020) considered as the legal structure to be adopted for the "future partnership", which – like those with Japan and Canada – should be designed to provide for *"mechanisms for dialogue, and, if necessary, dispute resolution"*, and should exclude any *"role for the Court of Justice of the European Union in the dispute resolution mechanism"* (Part 1, sec. 83).

Separate Markets: the EU-UK Trade and Cooperation Agreement

The contractual mechanism devised under the 2019 Agreement was vital to the similar provisions contained in the **EU-UK Trade and Cooperation Agreement** (TCA) signed on 24 December 2020, after an intense period of negotiations, and now regulating the commercial relationship between the Parties (basically referred to goods and, in a limited way, to services).

The **TCA** provides for a corresponding dispute settlement procedure that adopts the broad lines of the previous agreement, setting up – as stated by the **UK Government TCA Summary**– *"dispute resolution mechanisms that are appropriate for a relationship between sovereign equals"* that are *"fully reciprocal and equally available to both Parties"* (p. 30).

The framework is based on two consolidated lines: *consultation* (Part 6, Title I, art. 13), followed by *independent arbitration* (art. 14) in the event of disagreement, regulating the "*establishment of an arbitration Tribunal*" (art. 15), composed of three arbitrators, appointed by each party from a list of Arbitrators.

The chairperson would be agreed or appointed by the co-chair of the "**Partnership Council**" (that is part of the institutional framework, see *infra*). The **TCA** provides for the *function* of the arbitration tribunal (art. 17) and the *ruling* (art. 20) on the lines of the contractual-like arbitration procedures.

This **dispute settlement** mechanism applies to most areas of the *Trade and Cooperation Agreement* including level playing field, i.e. all the regulatory areas.

With regard to ***remedies***, if the arbitration panel finds that there has been a breach, either the breach is rectified or there will be *"suitable compensation"*. If neither way is pursued, the other Party can suspend obligations in response to any identified imbalance.

The procedures appear to give place to a credible and robust **enforcement** and **compliance mechanism** including the possibility of suspending the complaining party's obligations under the *Trade and Cooperation Agreement*, e.g. to reintroduce tariffs and quotas.

> *"Furthermore, each Party will under certain conditions be able to cross-retaliate whenever another Party does not comply with the ruling of the arbitration tribunal. For instance, a persisting breach by one Party that concerns a specific economic sector will allow the other Party to retaliate with measures in other economic sectors. Each Parts may also unilaterally take appropriate safeguard measures in cases of serious economic, societal or environmental difficulties of a sectorial or regional nature" [COM (2020) 856 final, 25.12.2020].*

The above quotation is an abstract of the comment on the relevant points by the EU Commission in its **Explanatory Memorandum** attached to the *Proposal for the Council Decision on the Trade and Cooperation Agreement* (TFEU art. 217). The wording used is very typical of the *contractual–like* legal nature of the **TCA**. While the *Principles of Interpretation* set out that the Agreement shall be interpreted *"in accordance with the customary rules of interpretation of public international law"* (Part 1, Title I, art. 13), terms such as *enforcement*, *obligation, retaliation* or *unilateral safeguards and measures* – recalled in an official Party's comment – all reveal mutual distrust requiring specific **contractual clauses** to protect reciprocal economic interest.

The **TCA** states in the *Preamble* the point making clear that for the Parties;

> *"it is essential to establish provisions ensuring overall governance, in particular dispute settlement and enforcement rules that fully respect the autonomy of the respective legal orders".*

The Parliamentary Role: the Condition Precedent

The **TCA** required parliamentary approval from the UK and the EU. The former was provided at the last minute of the expiration of the Transition period by the approval, in a one-day session (on 30 December 2020) of the ***EU (Future Relationship) Act*** to allow the agreement to take full legal effect from January 1, 2021. Since it was not possible to submit it to the European Parliament for approval by January 1, 2021, the EU gave provisional effect to the **Trade and Cooperation Agreement**. In terms of EU constitutional law the **TCA** deals only with EU competences (not interfering with those of Member States) so that it does not require ratification in the national parliaments (as it would have been, it was a so-called *mixed agreement*).

From another perspective, in the wider context of British constitutional law, the parliamentary role in the UK's exit was not clearly carved in stone.

Constitutional theorists have rather contributed during the process to clarify the point.

According to the "private law" language typically used by a contractual agreement, the parliamentary acts necessary for withdrawal can be conceived of as a "**condition precedent**" in a twofold sense:

> *"statutory authorization at the first stage ensures parliamentary voice as a condition precedent to initiating withdrawal, since the impact on rights may be felt to be too far-reaching to warrant inception of withdrawal talks at all; statutory authorization at the second stage ensures such parliamentary voice as a condition precedent for concluding withdrawal, since it thereby enables Parliament to make a fully-informed assessment as to the desirability of the withdrawal agreement when the actual impact on rights is known".* [P. CRAIG, in F. FABBRINI (2017)].

The first "condition precedent" (to "initiate withdrawal") was in itself – as is well known – the result of an internal UK debate on whether or not *"the constitutional requirements"* required a *parliamentary vote* authorizing notification to the EU of the withdrawal.

"The King hath no prerogative, but that which the law of the land allows him" was ruled in the Case of Proclamations in 1610. More

than four hundred years later, the High Court cited that ruling and affirmed the principle in the case raised *"about the UK constitutional process requirements to be satisfied before exit could begin"* [*(R. (Miller) v. The Secretary of State for Exiting the European Union [2016] EWHC 2768 (Admin)*].

The High Court stated:

> *"It is common ground that withdrawal from the European Union will have profound consequences in terms of changing domestic law in each of the jurisdictions of the United Kingdom"* [...]
> *"There is no superior form of law than primary legislation, save only where Parliament has itself made provision to allow that to happen. The ECA 1972, which confers precedence on EU law, is the sole example of this"*.

The Supreme Court upheld the ruling (*R (Miller) v Secretary of State for Exiting the European Union* [2017] UKSC 5 (2017)).

> *"The main issue on this appeal* [by the Secretary of State] *concerns the ability of ministers to bring about changes in domestic law by exercising their powers at the international level"*; *"ministers are not normally entitled to exercise any power they might otherwise have if it results in a change in UK domestic law, unless statute, i.e. an Act of Parliament, so provides. The argument against the Secretary of State is that this principle prevents ministers withdrawing from the EU Treaties, until effectively authorized to do so by a statute"*.

In this case – unlike the dissolution of international treaties – withdrawal had immediate effects on domestic law, precisely because EU membership implies *recognition* of *EU primacy*.

As has been noted

> *"the judgments were no less than a full judicial tour of the historical foundations of the division of powers between the legislature and the executive"* [P. EECKHOUT, in B. MARTILL *et al.* (2018)].

However, seen through the eyes of a continental lawyer, what was most relevant to this "judicial tour" is that the primacy of EU law was accepted by the UK courts only at the moment of exit from the European Union.

As for the referendum itself, it had *advisory* nature. In terms of constitutional theory, the *"distinction popularized by Dicey"* [G. Marshall, G.C. Moodie (1971)] between *"legal sovereignty"* (Parliament) and *"political sovereignty"* (the electorate) remains well established (*"the political supremacy of the electorate is still acknowledged as a limitation upon the exercise of legislative power"*) [E.C.S. Wade, *Introduction to A.V. Dicey* (1958)].

Parliament's role in the withdrawal process has – notoriously – enlivened the British political debate with the implementation of the "second condition precedent" ("parliamentary voice […] for concluding withdrawal"), stalling the process for about one year. This debate confirmed, however, the fundamental principle of the doctrine of parliamentary sovereignty: a cornerstone of "English legal education", which from T. Hobbes (Magdalen Hall) to A.V. Dicey (Balliol) has been *"almost entirely the work of Oxford men"* [R.T. Houston (1961)] and which – according to some authors – in modern times is paving the way in the UK legal system for *"a constitutional moment"* [V. Bogdanor (2019)], a theme that would take a continental author far from his permitted path.

Perspectives on the New Partnership

The signing of the **TCA** and its parliamentary ratification through the **EU "Future Partnership" Act** 2020 represents the dawn of this new cycle in the history of the relationship.

The issues at stake are various and complex. From the angle adopted for this survey, the focus in the following chapters is on the implications – in terms of **Legacy (Part I), Regulation (Part II)** and **Policy (Part III)** – of the wording with which the **Political Declaration** *"setting out the framework for the future relationship between the EU and the UK"*, signed by the Parties on 17 October 2019, defined the economic and legal prospects for the future relationship: **separate markets and distinct legal orders**.

"Identity" marks the distinctiveness of the two legal order; in terms of potential discontinuity for the UK; "*consistency*" for the EU with the **integrity** and **autonomy** of the Union's **legal order** as restated by the EU Commission in its **Explanatory Memorandum**:

> *"these agreements will not require the Union to amend its rules, regulations or standards in any regulated area" [p. 2].*

"Separate markets" means that the quest for "identity" will have to be transformed from a **moral idea** into an **economic issue**.

The aim of this book is to investigate how the legal orders will provide the **regulatory framework** for separate markets, to understand the effects of **reciprocal influences** and the **intellectual debt** that each vision owes to the other, and to what extent the respective **visions** remain different in the current post–Brexit era.

Within this limited but significant scope of work, assumptions can be verified by looking beyond the awkwardness of the Brexit process, and asking our contemporary legal minds whether a "European" institutional culture can help to look *"into the future of a common past"* [G. GALASSO, in AMATO *et al.* (2019)].

Looking back at the intellectual **heritage**, a classic study on "parliamentary government in England", remarks that

> *"every period of rapid social change confronts the danger that its legal habits may not keep pace with the political decisions it has to interpret"* [H.J. LASKI (1938)].

This is an everlasting reflection valid in our times, especially at a time when "*rapid social change*" requires that "**legal habits**" keep pace – once again – with the more radical political decisions taken in the European context since the birth of the European Union, leading to *new distinct European legal orders*.

Part 1

LEGACY

Chapter 1
ORIGINS

"It is necessary to form a treaty to which all the principal parties of Europe should bind themselves to protect and support each other as a general system of public law in Europe"
(WILLIAM PITT, THE YOUNGER, 1805)

Intellectual Legacy

It may seem paradoxical that the idea of a treaty among the main European parties, establishing a general system of public law, was the vow of an English statesman who lived in the age of global Britain, i.e. in the era of the maximum deployment of the concepts of sovereignty and national identity. It is much less paradoxical if we consider that the idea did not – in William Pitt's words – involve Great Britain.

From a more remote historical point of view, the EU's modern "general system of public law" geographically coincides (apart from Poland, some northern countries and some German "Länder") with the ancient Roman Empire and this coincidence also embraces the UK, although limited to England and Wales.

English legal history actually begins with Roman Britain. For four centuries England was an integral part of a single political and institutional system:

> *"Alongside and allied to this is the fact that it was a world dominated by the rule of law, which closely regulated the relations between the individual and the State and between one man and another"* [P. SALWAY (1981)].

As is often said, law is a language and the Roman heritage is still perceived today through language.

*Since the origins of the history of European nations, in constructing their legal systems both continental and Anglo-Saxon languages have used terms inherited from the Latin world "**ius**":*

> *"à partir de ius s'est forgé tout un vocabulaire qui passera du latin aux langues européennes avec la renaissance médiévale du droit romain dans les universités"* [S. KERNEIS (2018)].

Terms like "jurisdiction", "judge", "juridique", "judiciary", "jurisprudence" and "justice" have equivalents in all European languages: a semantic legacy witnessed by ancient documents such as the writing of the Magna Carta. It was precisely on "Latin" words that the legitimacy of fiscal power was formulated: fiscal power could not be levied except "per commune consilium regni nostri", clause 12 ("[…] by the common counsel of our realm") [A. ARLIDGE, I. JUDGE (2014)].

This is an inheritance witnessed also by the name of the constitutional writ aimed at challenging unlawful detention: habeas corpus ad subjiciendum (the full name – as pointed out by the main authorities – "betraying its venerable origin" [T. BINGHAM (2010)]. Analogously, later the Petition of Rights (1628) clarified that its rules derived from the "legem terrae": contemporary authors note that those rules already included "elements of substantive law and procedural propriety" [D.J. GALLIGAN (1996)].

On the other hand,

> *"les difficultés des juristes à construire un droit européen illustrent bien sûr la diversité des cultures juridiques […] de l'attachement des nations à leurs droits et aux traditions qui les fondent"* [S. KERNEIS (2018)].

In the complex scenario of different legal traditions, l'"affaiblissement de la culture latine" represents an original historical mark de la diversité juridique of the British Isles.

Historians note that the oldest Anglo-Saxon legislative sources belong to the rules of Kent (VII century) and "contrairement aux lois du continent rédigées en latin" [S. KERNEIS (2018)] the rules are written in the old English language.

The documents written in Latin survived through universities and the Inns of Courts until the 15th century: "the first translations [of the Magna Carta] into English date from this period" [A. LYON (2019)]. But the early formation, from the 12th century onwards, of a national system of law (Common Law) implied a more limited influence of Roman law in England than on the continent, with the exception of the ecclesiastical courts "which clung to the vestiges of Roman Law" [B. ABEL-SMITH, R. STEVENS (1967)]:

> *"from the middle or end of the thirteenth century, no lawyer in an English Common law court, for example, would have thought to build an argument on texts drawn from Roman Law"* [J. BELL, C. KILPATRICK (2006)].

On the other hand, on the continent in the 11th century, the rediscovery in Italy of ancient Roman law instead nurtured the foundations of what was the beginning of a "European legal science based on the study of the compilation of Roman law" [R. LESAFFER (2009)] and which, thanks to the confluence of Roman and Canon law, gave rise to what was known as ius commune.

It is not surprising, therefore, that over time the advocates of a European private law system ("the common private law of Europe") sought links with historical traditions, especially recalling the peculiar amalgam of learned law given by ius commune. The end of the 15th century marked the resolution in favour of learned law throughout Europe, but with the clear exception of England.

At that time the distinction was already clear.

> *"'Civilian' was the term commonly used to describe English lawyers trained in the Roman hand canon laws whose careers were spent in the several courts where the European ius commune provided the principal source of substantive and procedural law"* [R.H. HELMOLTZ, in D. IBBETSON *et al.* (2019)].

Historians have often stressed the hostility towards "civilians" felt by most English common lawyers. On the other hand, the issue is even more complex if one looks at the foundations of the various sources of English law.

From this point of view

> *"so far as there is any consistent theory of custom at all in Roman Law, it is clearly relegated to a subordinate position among the sources of law"* [C.K. ALLEN (1964)].

A broader question, however, is its influence in the foundation of the doctrine of precedent or "how far Roman Law directly inspired the beginnings of our equitable jurisdiction" [Ibid].

The topic is very broad and embraces the history of relations between common law and ius commune. For our purposes it will be sufficient to note that:

> *"Durant les siècles qui suivirent, ils divergèrent pour former deux grandes familles, celle des droits issus de ce que les juristes anglo-saxons considèrent être Civil Law, le droit romain, et celle des droits de Common Law, un droit des juges prétendu coutumier. L'opposition allait durer, elle divise aujourd'hui l'Europe"* [S. KERNEIS (2018)].

The gap in intellectual origins was widened by the European civil codification process in the early 19th century. The "codification" movement was re-

jected by the common law tradition, which was formed on the grounds of private law based on custom and case law rather than on a code.

From the specific point of view of public law, the original elements that characterized English "patterns of institutional notions" [P. CANE (2009)] may be traced back to the Middle Ages as well. Sporadic traces of a single remote language can also be found in legal terms of public law: e.g. the evolution of the concept of ultra vires to denote an excess of authority by independent statutory bodies or the notion of locus standi in the judicial review to indicate the legal capacity to challenge an administrative decision.

These are limited examples reflecting common origins but stemming from a remote past. Although they apparently recall "vieilles categories fondamentales public/privè", they leave traces that even today continue to inspire visions (infra Ch. 2) and that determine the foundations (infra Ch. 3) of the current relationship

> *"entre droit et économie dans l'élaboration de la norme ou bien encore de la concurrence entre Civil Law et Common Law à travers notamment le projet de construction d'un droit européen"* [S. KERNEIS (2018)].

The age of "accession"

Given the remote traces of a **single legal system of public law, it is only in contemporary times**, and particularly in the last forty-six years, that a historical period has given rise to a general system of public law in Britain and continental Europe.

Our contemporary era marks a historical shift in the construction of a single system of public law even for the main continental countries. The new age, an **age of accession,** began in 1957 and lasted until the beginning of the 20th century (2004). It was characterized by the continuous enlargement of EU "boundaries" due to new accessions, from the six initial founders (France, Germany, Italy and the Benelux countries) to the 28 EU Member States. An extension of boundaries that was

> *"to become larger than the Roman Empire, let alone the Holy Roman Empire, had ever been. It now includes countries that had not been part of either, and indeed countries that never accepted the aim of a federation, like Britain. The effect is undoubtedly one of overstretch, not only in physical and financial terms, but also in terms of having brought in societies where the values of the old members are not fully shared"* [B. HEUSER (2019)].

The economic legal order

In this context, the sole certain and unifying assumption among Member States is given by the European Union as an "economic legal order", opened by the *Treaty of Rome* (1957) and introducing the elements of the Common Market, the *Single European Act* (1986) developing the tools of the single market itself and the *Treaty of Maastricht* (1992) providing new instruments for financial, budgetary and stability regulation.

The economic objectives were (since the very origins) part of political objectives, the latter being oriented towards the establishment of *general* political power: a **political project** with emotional roots, deeper than the economic rationale shared (at least initially) by the original founders.

Further and consistent developments in this direction led to the elaboration of the *European Constitution* by the convention established by the Declaration of Laeken on the "*Future of the European Union*" (December 2001) and chaired by Valery Giscard d'Estaing. This text, including substantial modifications (necessary for approval by all EU Member States) became part of the treaty establishing a "*Constitution for Europe*" which was solemnly signed (as the 1957 Treaty) in Rome on 29 October 2004.

The "Constitution" was aimed at a European *political* – as well as economic – *order* in which issues of *institutional architecture* regarding executive and parliamentary powers would have had a fundamental role. It was the highest expression of a process that led – at the time – French and British comparativists to observe that

> *"la tradition juridique française* [...] *considèrent avec une sympathie naturelle la constitutionnalisation croissante de l'Union Européenne et de son système juridique, alors que la tradition juridique et la culture politique anglaises continuent à préférer nettement le constitutionnalisme informel et non écrit"* [J-B. Auby, M.R. Freedland, in M.R. Freedland, J-B. Auby (2006)].

In fact, the assumed *sympathie naturelle* was not – even at the time – shared by the people's will in France either, to the extent that the ratification process was blocked by the negative results of the French referendum in May 2005.

The new version of the economic constitution shifted in the *Lisbon Treaties* (2007), which renounced the aim of European political governance.

Rather than being founded on concepts of sovereignty, EU **governance** proved to be based on procedures of negotiation, bargaining, sector agreements and joint decision-making. However, a *"general system of public law"*, which basically concerns economic issues, was firmly rooted in the two treaties: *the Treaty on European Union* (TEU) and the *Treaty on Functioning of European Union* (TFEU) (hereinafter, together the "**Treaties**"), in force since 2009, which define the EU's current *legal and economic order.*

"Archaeological Diggings"

On the other side of the Channel, already in 1946 – just a year after the end of the war – Churchill in his famous Zurich speech called for the creation of a "*kind of United States of Europe*".

> *"At present there is a breathing-space. The cannons have ceased firing. The fighting has stopped; but the dangers have not stopped. If we are to form the United States of Europe or whatever name or form it may take, we must begin now"* [*www.churchill-society-london.org.uk/astonish-html*]

Despite Churchill's ringing call, the UK stood aside from the process when it started a few years later. *"Indeed, Churchill himself was clear that the UK would encourage but not join European integration"* [J. PEET, A. LA GUARDIA (2014)] (since the beginning envisaged as a partnership between France and Germany), with the UK acting rather as "friend and sponsor" of that partnership and not as a fully participating member.

Public opinion itself was not very interested in the steps taken in that direction during the run-up to the Messina conference which set six European nations on course to establish a single market. One British minister's abrupt dismissal of the preparatory meeting (Messina, 1954) for the forthcoming Treaty of Rome as *"archaeological diggings"* was followed by a similar attitude in the English-speaking press:

> *"the treaty's-signing ceremony in the Palazzo dei Conservatori on Rome's Capitoline Hill did not make the front pages in the English-speaking press. "Common Market Draft Signed" said the headline on a short piece relegated to page seven of the following day's Financial Times"* [P. STEPHENS, *Europe's fight to prove union has staying power after Brexit*, in *Financial Times,* 15 March 2017].

The constitutional terms

This attitude changed in the 1960s when the British government decided to get more involved, but notoriously France (on the assumption that the UK was more interested in its special relationship with the USA) vetoed the

British entry twice, *malgré* the expectations of the other five members of the (then) *European Economic Community* (EEC).

The decision to join was successful with Edward Heath's government: the UK signed the Treaty of Rome and joined the EEC on 1 January 1973. The decision was confirmed by the referendum held in 1975 and the country – in astonishing contrast to the "second" referendum that would take place four decades later – voted two to one in favour of staying.

In legal terms, after accession, UK **constitutional history** was strongly marked by **institutional confirmations.**

The list of Parliament acts defining the terms of membership opened with the (1972) *European Community Act* (ECA) and continued with the *European Parliamentary Election Act* (1978) which enshrined the fundamental principle:

> *"No treaty which provides for any increase in the powers of the European Parliament shall be ratified by the United Kingdom unless it has been approved by an Act of Parliament"* (sec. 6).

Since then the steps in the construction of the contemporary European Union included, on the British side, a relevant devolution of powers at the European level, all approved by Parliament, starting with the *European Communities (Amendment) Act* 1986, which implements the *Single European Act.*

Then the *European Communities* (*Amendment*) Act 1993 implemented the *Maastricht Treaty* (it is – to our contemporary eyes – significant that the *parliamentary motion* designed to approve the *Maastricht bill* passed on 4 November 1992, but the vote was with a majority of only three votes).

Subsequently, the European Union (*Amendment*) Act 2008 implemented the *Lisbon Treaties.*

With the aforementioned Parliamentary acts the UK became part of the common **system of public** regulatory law, even though throughout its membership the UK enjoyed – as is well known – a "specific situation" characterized by a wide range of exemptions and derogations from EU policies resulting in a partially different *status* from that of the other Member States.

Those exemptions and derogations appeared to be made for tactical, political or economic reasons. In fact, behind them there was a much more significant background, both in terms of historical roots of **legal traditions** and in terms of **a conflict of ideas**.

Since the very beginning of its membership, the British approach has aimed at a **commercial transaction**: a membership motivated by economic circumstances rather than political choices, but nevertheless – as we will see – a very **influential membership** in **intellectual terms**.

From the *Withdrawal Agreement* and the *Political Declaration* to the current negotiations on the "new partnership"

Recent constitutional history turned the page with Parliament's approval of the *European Union Referendum Act* 2015, which enabled the British people to be "consulted" on a single binary question: *"Should the United Kingdom remain a member of the European Union or leave Europe?"*

The subsequent constitutional chapter opened with the *European Union (Notification of Withdrawal) Act (2017)* approved by the British Parliament on 13 March 2017, which authorized the government to notify its exit from the European Union, and consequently to start negotiations to that end.

Later, Parliament approved the *European Union (Withdrawal) Act 2018* passed in June 2018, which allows the government to convert EU law into domestic law with the aim of avoiding *"any sudden or unpredictable uncertainty"*. The Act amends the **sources of law** by internalising EU rules as national rules. The "conversion" operation – technically qualified as "retaining" legislation (*supra* Introduction) –will make it possible, from time to time, to modify or repeal EU law through parliamentary statutes or delegated legislation.

Finally, on 17 October 2019, the UK and the 27 EU members (Council Decision (EU) 2019/1750) approved the *"Agreement on the Withdrawal of the United Kingdom of Great Britain and Northern Ireland from the European Union and the European Atomic Energy Community"*.

The withdrawal process was completed on the UK side in legislative terms with the – already mentioned – approval of the *European Union (Withdrawal) Act 2020* of 23 January 2020 and, on the EU side, with the *European Parliament Legislative Resolution* of 29 January 2020.

The **Withdrawal Agreement** essentially focused on regulating the transition period from exit day to the "transition period completion day" provided for in the Agreement (Article 126) on 31 December 2020. The Agreement also provided for an *"extension of the transition period"* of up to one or two years (Art. 132 (1)) by decision of the *Joint Committee* established for the governance of the Agreement itself.

However, it was agreed that the UK, after exit day, would not participate *"in any enhanced cooperation"* (Article 127 (4)).

On the same date of the **Withdrawal Agreement**'s approval, the parties signed a non-binding document: the *"Political Declaration setting out the* *framework for the future relationship between the EU and the UK".*

The Parties agreed that as a general rule, during the transition period EU law

> *"shall produce in respect of and in the United Kingdom the same legal effects as those which it produces within the Union and its Member States, and shall be interpreted and applied in accordance with the same methods and general principles as those applicable within the Union"* [Withdrawal Agreement, Article 127(3)].

A previous agreement had been – notoriously – negotiated and signed by the parties one year earlier (on 25 November 2018) but – as is also well known – was not ratified by the British Parliament.

The revised **Withdrawal Agreement** signed in October 2019 seems to present few changes (mainly due to necessary technical adaptations to the new customs regime of Northern Ireland). In real terms, it actually contains significant differences as to the perspectives of the two (UK and EU) economies due to the removal of provisions on the *level playing field* commitments with regard to issues such as *competition*, *state aid*, *public procurement*, etc.

The commitments were intended – in the previous agreement – to limit the UK's capacity to obtain what can be considered an unfair advantage by lowering standards.

> *"The level playing field provisions were in the area of taxation, environmental protection, labour standards, state aid and competition. These have now been replaced by less specific and not-binding commitments in the Political Declaration to uphold such principles in any future trade agreements between the EU and the UK"* [Commons Library (2019)].

The point appears to be the crucial issue of the *envisaged new partnership* called for in the **political declaration**.

The differences are reflected in the official documents defining the position of the parties at the beginning of the negotiations for the **new partnership**.

The EU position was set out in the EU Council's *Directives for Negotiation of a new partnership with the United Kingdom*, 25 February 2020 (**Directives for Negotiation**), while the UK's position was represented by the *UK's Approach to Negotiations – The Future Relationship with the EU,* 27 February 2020 [UK's Approach to Negotiations].

The two official positions were followed by the *Draft text of the Agreement on the New Partnership with the United Kingdom* (published on 18 March 2020) [**EU Draft Text**], issued by the European Commission (specifically, by the Task Force for Relations with the United Kingdom), and by the *Draft Working Text for a Comprehensive Free Trade Agreement between the United Kingdom and the European Union* [**UK Draft**] as the respective negotiating documents of the parties.

The true effects of the United Kingdom's secession stem from certain unshared commitments and diverging "negotiating documents". The **shared values** then helped mitigate the uncertainties implicit in the new prospects.

Chapter 2
VISIONS

"We shall not cease from exploration
And the end of all our exploring
Will be to arrive where we started
And know the place for the first time"
(T.S. ELIOT, Little Gidding)

Shared Legacy and Ordre Économique

T. S. Eliot's emblematic verse reminds the reader that any new path reflects the strength of heritage. ***Intellectual legacy*** *in our context remains the basis of the perspective of what the "future of the common past" will be.*

In modern times, the ***continental*** *"general system of public law" dates back to the 1930s with the enucleation and emergence of a new space, aimed at defining and identifying the foundations – and limits – of* ***economic interventionism****.*

At the time, on the basis of 18th *century state science ("Staatswissenschaft") German thinkers developed ideas known as* ***ordoliberalism*** *(or the Freiburg School) by applying those ideas to a growing range of economic and social problems. In the words of German economists:*

> *"According to the new doctrine, rules needed to be formulated in general terms and the state's actions should be confined to the enforcement of such general laws, for instance, the laws on competition and against cartels, which had been an important part of the older German tradition of business management. Unlike Hayek, who more and more insisted on the spontaneous creation of order and rules, the Ordoliberals emphasized the need for an initial elaboration of an appropriate framework"* [M.K. BRUNNERMEIER, H. JAMES, J.P. LANDAU (2016)].

The Freiburg economists saw their ideal as a compromise between the extremes of an unregulated free market and unlimited state command: in this way they paved the way to the new concept of ***social market economy*** *("soziale Marktwirtschaft"). Accordingly, it followed that:*

> *"a genuine, equitable, and smoothly functioning competitive system cannot in fact survive without a judicious moral and legal framework and without regular supervision of the conditions under which competition can take place pursuant to real efficiency principles. This presupposes mature economic discernment on the part of all responsible bodies and individuals and a strong impartial state"* [*Ibid*].

Multiple confirmations of the non-existence of a state-market dichotomy derived, at the time, from the experience of other continental countries, primarily France:

> *"L'ordolibéralism écarte les conceptions classiques de «la main invisible» au profit d'une régulation étatique"* [A. GAILLET, in G. KALFLECHE *et al.* (2018)].

References to the set-up of ***institutions*** *capable of reconciling, as far as possible, the interests of individuals with the general interest, are widespread in contemporary works of economists.*

As the French Nobel prize winner J. Tirole highlights:

> *"the market economy is not an end in itself"* [...]*"the state's new role is to establish ground rules, to intervene when markets fail, to ensure healthy competition, to regulate monopolies, to supervise the financial system, to create true equality of opportunity, and to redistribute resources through taxation"* [...] *"Our choice of society is not between the state and the market, as partisans of state intervention and those of laissez-faire polices would have us believe. The state and the market are complementary, not mutually exclusive. The market needs regulation; the state needs competition and incentives"* [J. TIROLE (2017)].

Further recent economic literature confirms the assumption:

> *"Traditionally, markets have been presented as an alternative: either the state or the market proves to be the best way of organizing a given economic activity or set of choices. But this is a misleading way of thinking about how societies can collectively use the available resources to achieve the best possible outcomes for their members"* [D. COYLE (2020)].

This approach is shared by social theorists. Markets often function as "pivot et poumon d'une économie marchande [A. MINC (2012)]", but markets and the state could not exist without each other, at least in the form we know today:

> *"Le marché ne peut fonctionner correctement sans un état de droit ; l'état de droit ne peut être appliqué et respecté sans un État"* [J. ATTALI (2011)].

Technology, economies and finance have never developed without a legal system that made it possible or facilitated the establishment of business, trade and contractual relations:

> *"ces objectifs nécessitent que le marché soit régulé ("ordo") et que les règles soient observées, et ceci implique un rôle beaucoup plus important du droit par rapport à des modèles qui se concentrent sur le pouvoir discrétionnaire des organes politiques"* [M. RUFFERT, in G. KALFLECHE *et al.* (2018)].

*As a result, "**growth**" is not achieved through the provision of additional money, but through **structural reforms**: a rigorous approach to **governing debt** and its limits is implicit. Recurring virtue – or austerity – is (according to the assumptions) rewarded by future benefits: stronger **rules** rather than shared **risks**.*

The Economic Constitution

The **intellectual foundations** of the EU's economic constitution may therefore be found (albeit not exclusively) in the concept of **social market economy.**

From this perspective, the economic dimension of Europe is particularly significant. What emerges after more than six decades is a single market without internal economic borders. It is an area previously characterized by customs barriers to the movement of services, capital, people and goods, and by almost exclusively national markets, as well as economic planning, and currencies with strictly national monetary policies.

However, the peculiarity of all this is that the **economic dimen-**

sion is based on a **vision** formally recognized and constitutionalized in the treaties of reconciling divergent priorities and a **heterogeneity of political values** among members. It is a vision or in other words **a platform of ideas** underlying the *pattern* of political relations in Europe. The Union endeavours to achieve:

> *"sustainable development of Europe based on balanced economic growth and price stability, a highly competitive social market economy, aiming at full employment and social progress"* [TEU, Article 3(3)].

The constitutional implications underpin the notion of the *"internal market as a legal concept"*. Consequently:

> *"In economic terms, the EU is intended to be a single space, unfragmented by national frontiers – which is a bold vision given the centuries of regulatory diversity, political division and cultural heterogeneity that has shaped the European continent* [...] *Accordingly the EU's commitment made by Article 3(3) TEU to the establishment of an internal market carries constitutional significance"* [S. WEATHERILL (2017)].

The place assigned to the *market* in this vision is confirmed by the words *highly competitive* but also by the following words oriented to the *values* of *social cohesion.* This balance has concrete legal relevance in different regulated areas such as *public goods, networks, services,* and *infrastructure* (as will be seen in the next chapters).

More generally, the concept of an EU market economy suggests – more than an array of certainties – the tensions and possible **combinations** of **values** synthesized in the apparently **contradictory words** of "*social market economy*".

L'Ordre Économique

The result was (and, in fact, is) an ***economic constitution.*** Its elements were not generated by the simple transposition to the European level of the experiences of the single Member States. Rather, they mostly derive from the peaks reached by the Union and then applied to the legal systems of the Member States, giving rise to an original and autonomous *general system of public law.*

The notion of "economic constitution" was historically present in the German legal language (*Wirtschaftsverfassung*) and was later taken over by the French legal language (*la Constitution économique européenne*).

A concept of positive law includes "constitutive" and "regulatory" principles.

> *"The basic principles in the economic constitution would be both 'constitutive' (fundamental norms such as stability of the currency and private property) and 'regulative', to implement the more fundamental norms, notably through competition law. Thus, for the ordoliberals, the major constitutional questions included the balance between the private, market realm and that of the state, something needing explicit consideration in countries such as Germany with a more developed state tradition than the UK"* [T. PROSSER (2014)].

The aforementioned normative principles recall the theoretical foundations, fully acknowledged in continental literature:

> *"C'est bien dans ce sens de cadre institutionnel et juridique régulateur qu'il faut entendre la notion de «constitution» ou d'«ordre» économique. L'originalité de cette approche tient en conséquence à ce qu'elle s'envisage comme une troisième voie entre le «lasser-faire» du libéralisme classique et des formes plus «administrées» de l'économie"* [A. GAILLET, in G. KALFLECHE *et al.* (2018)].

Plural visions

Despite the solidity of the theoretical foundations, the internal process of building the European Union retains *differences in the underlying constitutional visions*, involving economic and even legal, political, and social aspects among the founding Member States. What emerges today, more than enthusiastic support for the alleged existence of *"a fairly compact constitutional object"*, [R. SCHÜTZE (2015)] is a **plurality of visions** of the economic constitution.

The plural concepts of economic constitutions are certainly linked to the straightforward differences between the interests of the founding EU Member States, in particular France and Germany.

Differences between European countries are often centred on

divergences in the **economic** area. The Treaty of Rome itself was the result of a Franco-German compromise:

> *"D'un côté, un étatisme social qui parfois se méfie de la théorie et de la pratique des marchés; de l'autre côté, une empreinte ordo-libérale fondée sur l'économique sociale du marché"* [G. KALFLECHE *et al.* (2018)].

Legacy and interests currently lay the foundations *"d'une analyse actuelle de la Constitution économique"* largely in the hands of France and Germany, the two Member States – despite serious elements of divergence – inevitably responsible *"pour l'avenir"* of the Union.

"The best of both worlds"

As regards the United Kingdom, the constitutional aspects of **accession** have been characterized throughout its membership period by an effort to combine maximum economic benefits with minimum loss of **sovereignty**:

> *"Ever since, the relationship between the United Kingdom and the European Union has remained complex. Fundamentally opposed to the idea of a 'federal' Europe, the United Kingdom has consistently favoured an ever-wider over an ever-deeper European Union; and while the British government has traditionally supported the liberalisation of the common market, it has been deeply critical towards European market regulation"* [R. SCHÜTZE, in R. SCHÜTZE *et al.* (2018)].

Longstanding expectations (not only from the UK) to reduce excessive EU regulation and create a **diverse range of national participation models** have been at the heart of the long list of derogations and exceptions (*opt-out clauses*) safeguarding the United Kingdom's membership.

As has been said with regard to the historical background of Brexit:

> *"Brexit did not emerge out of nowhere: it is the culmination of events that have been under way for decades and have historical roots stretching back well beyond that"* [K. O'ROURKE (2018)].

Before the culmination of events leading to the 2016 referendum, the EU-UK **settlement** of February 2016 [*Decision of the Heads of State or Government, meeting within the European Council, concerning a new settlement for the United Kingdom within the European Union,* European Council Conclusions (18-19 February 2016)] sought to provide an institutional framework for the conflict of ideas underlying these worlds.

The Settlement conceptualized the notion of *"the best of both worlds",* elaborating *"the United Kingdom's special status in a reformed European Union".*

On this basis, the UK's **special status** consisted mainly of not being engaged in an "*ever closer union*". The idea arose from the general recognition that an ever closer union was to be interpreted as *non-binding* for the UK, to make it clear that further political choices did not apply to the UK at all:

> *"It is recognized that the United Kingdom, in the light of the specific situation it has under the Treaties, is not committed to further political integration into the European Union. The substance of this will be incorporated into the Treaties at the time of their next revision in accordance with the relevant provisions of the Treaties and the respective constitutional requirements of the Member States, so as to make it clear that the references to ever closer union do not apply to the United Kingdom"* (sec. C (1)).

The **settlement** confirmed the European Council Conclusions 26-27 June 2014 which stated:

> *"the concept of ever closer union allows for different paths of integration for different countries, allowing those that want to deepen integration to move ahead, while respecting the wish of those who do not want to deepen any further"* [sec. III, par. 27].

The **settlement** could be the end of the story formalising (through *constitutional status*) a specific and long-lasting **unique kind of membership** within the framework of the Treaties, probably destined to be imitated by other Member States (especially non-Eurozone Members).

This would have meant – in such a case – opening up a constitutional debate on the different (formally recognized) *classes of membership* in the Union, paving the way for a wider debate on the different circles within the European Union. A debate that would have been destined to become a political one at European level, requiring in some Member States a popular vote*"according to the respective constitutional requirements"* – as established by the **settlement** – and the consequent *"revision of the relevant provisions of the Treaties"*.

From this point of view, it would have been the beginning of a new attempt (after the aborted 2004 "*Constitution for Europe*") at a European constitutional process. Instead, it was the *end of the beginning* and, in any case, the beginning of the **secession** of the first departing EU Member.

Values and Interests

Almost four years later (19.10.2019), the **Political Declaration** aimed – on a very different basis – to set out the **framework** for the **future relationship** between the European Union and the United Kingdom. Emblematically based on the *"international order"* (sec. 2), the resulting framework acknowledges that

> *"this relationship will be rooted in the values and interests that the Union and the United Kingdom share. These arise from their geography, history and ideals anchored in this common European heritage"* (sec. 3)

The statement is both a realistic (*"values and interests"*) and idealistic (*"ideals anchored in this common European heritage"*) interpretation of the common past.

It is evident that ***intellectual origins*** remain at the heart of the relevant issues of our time. Both **diverging** and **common** long-term historical, intellectual and cultural visions are at stake, intertwining continental and Anglo-Saxon economic visions and legal concepts. **Interests** are often interpreted through the lens of **ideas**. Some countries have developed their own economic traditions and schools of thought: given their historical paths, *different countries* in Europe follow *different legal* and *economic philosophies*.

The ***Political Declaration*** seems to take into account the complexity of the relationship between*"core values and rights"*. For this reason, the section *"Initial Provisions"* is dedicated to them, assuming, for the *"Basis for cooperation"*, **shared values** as

> *"an essential prerequisite for the cooperation envisaged in this framework" (sec. 6)*

The inspiration of a "*general system of public law*", is – in our contemporary time – still at the centre of the challenge foreseen a long time ago.

An "English invention": Accountability

Conflicting visions cannot in fact eliminate the **common concepts** that originated with **Anglo-Saxon culture** and that in recent decades have been absorbed by the **European economic order**.

A clear example of this *cross-fertilization* is the legal concept of **accountability** in public and private corporate law. In the areas of *competition* or *state aid* – two central issues in the legal drafting of the **Trade and Cooperation Agreement** in force as of January 1, 2021 – the concept takes a dominant position as it characterizes the institutional *milieu* in which economic activity takes place.

The assumption that accountability is a **dominant value** recalls the fact that in contemporary societies a "corporate form" is the product of certain basic **legal features**. As stated in the well-known *The Anatomy of Corporate Law* in a comparative analysis of various jurisdictions (including France, Germany, Italy and the UK):

> *"we develop a framework that is independent of the jurisprudential idiosyncrasies of any particular jurisdiction, and is therefore generally applicable. This framework provides common categories and a common language ('gemeinsame Problemsprache')"* [P. DAVIES, in R. KRAAKMAN *et al.*, quotation from the 1st ed. (2004); 3rd ed., J. ARMOUR *et al.* (2017)].

In this common and broader framework, *accountability* is an expression with **English exclusivity**, that is, without an exact equivalent in other European languages.

The notion is more meaningful than the technical notion of "responsibility" commonly used in European legal terminology and suggests the existence of a variety of applications. In this sense, the sphere of public law implies forms of accountability which would not attract *"liability in contract or tort or any other area of private law"*, but rather a *"relational account"* closely associated with a *"framework of values"* [P. CANE (2002)].

The continuous process of "giving an account" (*"la responsabilité de rendu compte"*) is a concept for which continental lawyers owe a debt of gratitude to an *"English invention"*, that is *"not in use everywhere and, when it is found, is often an English import"* [C. HARLOW (2002)].

Even more clearly, referring to the literature on the point, Professor Harlow plainly states that:

> *"Italian, Spanish and French possess no equivalent for the term. All need to borrow the English word if they wish to indicate its portmanteau sense"* [C. HARLOW, in N. BAMFORTH, P. LEYLAND (2003)].

This "English invention" recalls the conflict between private and public interests and, at the same time, the need for **rules** to compose the **conflict** itself, resolving related disputes and reducing uncertainties:

> *"stress on the meaning to be given to words such as accountability, control or power allows us to escape from over-concern with external judicial control"* [P. LEYLAND, in P. LEYLAND *et al.* (1997)].

This approach paves the way for a system of **governance values**, in which – in addition to an *ethos of management* regulatory principles – "giving an account" of the conduct of business is required:

> *"'Accountability' is then not just another political catchword but also refers to concrete practices of being accountable"* [H. ADDINK (2019)].

In EU regulation, *conflict resolution* in corporate issues is not attributed to specific institutions, as is the case for the protection of other public interests in "competition" or "banking services". The potential conflict between "responsibility" and "autonomy" requires a *balance* between law and economics, and, more importantly, requires *trust*:

> *"Accountability does involve checking, but it cannot function without trust: trust in those calling to account, and some degree of trust in the information being supplied by those being called to account. Accountability simply involves striking a different balance between the two values"* [A.C.L. DAVIES (2001)].

Legal-social theorists point out in the present time that:

> "a *mark of the knowledge economy is its tendency to change the moral culture of production, heightening the level of trust* [...] *The market economy could then be understood as a form of cooperation among strangers* [...] *impossible when there is no trust*" [R.M. UNGER (2019)].

Accountability is the value through which certain chapters of public law can be read, the *fil rouge* linking regulatory principles, notably in the areas of *competition law* (*infra* Ch. 3) and *public goods* (*infra* Ch. 4).

Above all, it is the value underlying the *legal framework* set up by the **Trade and Cooperation Agreement** for the foreseeable future. Accountability provides the conditions in which two economies will have – as stated in the *Preamble* of the Agreement – *"fair and open competition"* together with a *"balanced economic partnership"* to ensure a high standard of "*technical cooperation*" in regulated sectors.

More than four decades of membership have produced mutual Anglo-Saxon and European influences and a terrain of **interaction** between *Anglo-Saxon* and *continental visions*.

Chapter 3
FOUNDATIONS

"We have no eternal allies,
and we have no perpetual enemies.
Our interests are eternal and perpetual,
and those interests it is our duty to follow"
(LORD PALMERSTON,
House of Commons, 1 March 1848)

Internal Market Legacy and Level Playing Field

This epigraph clearly refers to foreign policy, which Palmerston directed for fifteen years in the 19th century, but, outside its original context, it conveys a forging "self-perception as one of Britain as detached from the affairs of Europe" [B. HEUSER (2019)].

The interests, previously played on the chess board of foreign policy, came to be at stake – in the contemporary global world – in the field of ***competition****.*

*The European Council "Directives for the Negotiation of a new partnership with the UK" (hereinafter, the "****Directives for Negotiation****") – adopted by the Council on 25 February 2020 – stated that the "envisaged partnership" – after the Transition Period – shall have to be backed up by robust commitments ensuring*

"a level playing field for open and fair competition"(I, sec.17).

The official position revealed the suggestion (and fear) that the UK could take a competitive approach based on the ***downgrading*** *of the EU* ***regulatory approach****.*

From a different angle, it could be assumed that despite the UK's attraction to a "light touch approach" to regulation, the UK has a close link to a ***common area of values*** *in competition and state aid. This is also because these values have so far been vested by a "shared administration" at EU level with UK participation (through the European Competition Network). Nevertheless, on this point the wording of the* ***Political Declaration*** *actually denotes some ambiguity in relation to the parties' intention to retain*

> *"their autonomy and the ability to regulate economic activity according to the levels of protection each deems appropriate in order to achieve legitimate public policy objectives" (sec. 18).*

The way competition will be interpreted in light of ***legitimate public policy objectives*** *will in fact determine the forthcoming scenario for the two economies and the actual possibility of avoiding fiscal, social and environmental dumping.*

Once again, beyond the unpredictable future prospects, the cultural legacy remains the only absolute certainty in reshaping future relations, given that the common legal framework of the last decades is deeply ***indebted to the Anglo-Saxon legal culture****.*

It would be impossible to address the issue here in general terms: what this chapter seeks to do is to outline the ideas and practices, mustered in Anglo-Saxon ***legal language****, that have fertilized* ***EU concepts****, spreading their influence in the drafting of rules and institutional frameworks.*

The issue of "taking values seriously" [S. WEATHERILL (2016)] – which originated with the Anglo-Saxon conceptual approach – was channelled into the EU's regulatory approach, in particular as regards the procedural dimension:

> *"secularized societies express a variety of interests and values, which require complex balancing exercises"* and *"in order to make conflicts between such values manageable, we need acceptable procedures for conflict resolution"* [G. DELLA CANANEA (2016)].

Interests *and* ***procedures*** *are therefore the elements needed to achieve a shared approach to a* ***level playing field*** *and are the (only) real guarantee for this in the current scenario, when, predictably, the two economies become bitter and hardened competitors.*

Neutral Ownership and Golden Power

A starting point for the level playing field scenario is the concept of neutral (as opposed to "public" or "private") ownership of companies.

Taking into account the "origins", the historical prevalence of state-owned companies in Europe was justified by the fact that state-controlled companies were qualified, at least until the 1990s, by the aim of protecting collective interests, including socially necessary economic initiatives not undertaken by privates, or initiatives involving long-term returns.

In contemporary times, the "public company" and the role of government as "shareholder" have a more limited role (although not in all Member States: France – for instance – remains widely a state-owned *colbertist* economy, often imitated by Germany, Austria and other Member States).

In a broader sense, public ownership can no longer be used as a means of bailing out enterprises or private sector assets in difficulty. This is mainly due to market-based predilections of EU policies.

> *"At a constitutional level, by far the most important regime has been that of EU state aid law and policy. This sets out detailed and sometimes complex constraints on actions of Member States, which have effectively ruled out many traditional techniques of industrial policy such as large-scale nationalization with open-ended financial support"* [T. PROSSER (2014)].

Government control was previously exercised through shareholder power, but in practice corporate powers were supplemented by additional powers, not least because financial support was largely dependent on government decisions.

There was an immanent conflict between the government's desire for public companies to represent the "public interest" as part of general economic policy on the one hand, and – on the other hand – the autonomous policies that companies should pursue independently in the interest of stakeholders.

This conflict was at the core of the "privatisation" process.

In the UK, the *privatisation process* started in the 1980s, while in almost all others EU countries it followed only a decade later. The UK stimulus helped push the EU towards *market liberalisation*, economic openness and, supposedly, increased market efficiency: *inter alia*, the influential role played by British EU Commissioners Arthur Cockfield and then Leon Brittan in the late 1980s and 1990s is widely recognized (M. Sandbu, *Exit from single market closes a chapter UK did so much to write, Financial Times, 31 December 2020).*

In legal terms the privatisation process introduced the concept of **neutral ownership** (public or private) of a company, as currently defined in Article 285 TEU.

"Privatisations" thus led to the end of the "notion" of "public enterprise" as having a separate legal regime, in favour of a *neutral shareholder structure*.

The economic literature showed on an empirical basis, in various legal systems, a correlation between the spread of privatisation and the models of "protection" for investors and stakeholders: the strong development of privatisations strengthens protection of the different interests involved in privatised companies.

After the privatisation phase, governments usually introduced *special rights* in public limited companies – such as the Anglo-Saxon *golden share* or the French *action spécifique* – especially in those companies operating in sensitive sectors such as defence, transport, telecommunications, energy and other public services.

The reasons for introducing a golden share or (as later redefined) ***golden power*** to reserve special rights to the state (as lately disciplined by EU Regulation 2019/452) can be summarized as follows:

- the need to prevent that privatisation of public utilities, given the low competition factor that characterizes these sectors, would replace a public monopoly with a private one;
- the particular social relevance of these sectors, which require specific protection that cannot be left to market laws.

In normal times golden power is basically aimed at countering acquisitions by non-EU entities or companies with registered offices in the EU owned by non-EU entities.

In extraordinary times – such as those caused by the ***pandemic crisis*** in all national economies – the scope has also been extended to potential acquisition by companies with registered offices in other Member States (national regulations have been adopted in Germany, France, Spain and Italy), clearly affecting the very concept of the internal market. In fact, the **pandemic crisis** has caused one of the most intense periods of **state intervention** since the postwar period.

This initiative – like the one concerning renewed public intervention to rescue, through **state recapitalisation**, companies operating in economic sectors where the impact of the economic shock is heavier – must be considered (to maintain the original assumptions of a single market) temporary. Therefore they were placed by the EU in a specific **"Temporary Framework"**, resulting in a specific **mitigated state aid scheme** adopted by the EU Commission on 20 March 2020 and subsequently amended on 4 April, 8 May and 13 October 2020 (on which, *infra* in this chapter).

The Contemporary Foundations of Public Reason

The pandemic shock confirms that recurring crises reinforce the need for **new forms of public regulation**.

The term **corporate governance** commonly used in this context is an emblematic expression of the confluence of **private and public reason** in the operational logic of a company.

The path opened up by privatisation fostered the evolution of corporate law towards models of general public accountability.

Accountability, used in close association with *governance,* highlights (*supra* Ch. 2) the element of calling to account for choices made with a view to *transparency,* with reference to a clear objective of external evidence in the eyes of an active and informed civil community. **Economic rationality** must account for all the different forms of public responsibility with which corporate actors need to comply.

> *"So conceived, competition law may thus be regarded as an accountability mechanism – a means by which private actors can be called to account to the public for the way in which they exercise their market power"* [K. YEUNG, in M.R. FREEDLAND *et al.* (2006)].

In this context, Anglo-Saxons and continental lawyers found a common language in concepts such as *corporate social responsibility* (CSR), or more recently *environment, social, governance* (ESG), which include the protection of both the system as a whole and collective interests in relevant relations with the company itself (minority shareholders, financial institutions, employees, suppliers), or interests aimed at environmental, social and economic sustainability.

In order to go to the foundations, it is necessary to specify which values are intrinsic to the "private" and "public" reasons for the corporate system.

The "public" reason concerning general interests gives rise to **corporate regulation** which is in itself of a *public law* nature. The theories of public reason largely contributed to justifying *"the perceived inadequacy of theories of legitimacy"* based only on consent and the need to accept *"the social part of value pluralism"*.

To our ends:

> *"In general, public reason demands that moral or political principles be justifiable, or reasonably acceptable, to all those persons to whom the principles are meant to apply"* [J.L. MASHAW, in J. BELL, M. ELLIOT, J. NE VARUHAS (2016)].

In fact, when relations between parties go beyond contractual terms and the interests at stake shift from individual to general, the "contract" takes a step back.

The market is not a mere patchwork of contractual cases and is not simply ordered by a *lex mercatoria.* On the contrary, it requires continuous adjustments between *public* and *private regulation.* The result is the identification of underlying values of public law stemming from the mere fact that

> *"public bodies and private bodies exercising public or governmental functions possess many kinds of power, which do not have direct parallels normally in purely private relationships"* [M. TAGGART(1997)].

Therefore, conflict resolution cannot be fully delegated to the contract when it requires some kind of **general interest protection**. As is observed in the "classics" constitutional works:

> *"it is necessary, also, to prevent the possibility that the power of the company may be used, as has been the habit of corporate enterprise in the past, to the detriment of the public interest"* [H.J. LASKY (1925)].

"Public reason" in joint stock companies – incorporating a broader notion of accountability – recalls once again an English term, '*stakeholder*' with its **exclusive** propriety of meanings. This view is shared by continental authors:

> *"stakeholders" – "autre terme aujourd'hui sans traduction et qui décrit tous les groupes humains en interaction avec l'enterprise"* [A. MINC (2019)].

In its meaningful definition, it refers to

> *"parties affected by corporate activities but who lack any contractual leverage over the firm. We term such parties – who are not shareholders, managers, employees, or creditors – the firm's 'external constituencies'"* [R. KRAAKMAN, in J. ARMOUR *et al.* (2017)].

The need to be **accountable** towards these *"group humains an interaction avec l'enterprise"* or *"outside parties"* is the foundation of a perceived ***modèle Anglo-Saxon*** of the **market**, a *modèle* in which

> *"les règles de transparence, de respect des actionnaires, de responsabilité des conseils d'administration, de refus des contrôles rampants sont aussi exigeantes dans la réalité que dans le discours"* [A. MINC (2019)].

Once again, **western legal values** are indebted in contemporary times to Anglo-Saxon legal constructions.

Needless to say, the debt arose long ago, as the history of private companies began in Great Britain with the birth of the East India Company (24 September 1599), the first joint-stock company open to all investors:

> *"The idea of a joint stock company was one of Tudor England's most brilliant and revolutionary innovations. The spark of the idea sprang from the flint of the medieval crafts guilds, where merchants and manufactures could pool their resources to undertake ventures none could afford to make individually" [W. DALRYMPLE (2019)].*

The idea of "one corporate body" with a "legal identity" was therefore (another) British **invention**. The danger associated with unregulated private companies led the British Parliament at the time to support companies with state power, until they eventually turned into what we today might call public-private partnerships:

> *"Yet if history shows anything, it is that in the intimate dance between the power of the state and that of the corporation, while the latter can be regulated, the corporation will use all the resources in its power to resist"* [*Ibid*].

La **pratique britannique** is therefore a **legacy** for the various continental models, often differing from each other as witnessed by the difference between a *"système allemande coherent avec l'endogamie de la classe dirigente"* and *"le modèle francais"* enriched by a high level of foreign direct investment, but still burdened by *"la place exorbitante du secteur public"* [A. MINC (2019)], certainly not destined to be reduced in the short term.

Competition as a Dominant Value

The perennial need for the business world to be guided by standards of fair conduct enlightens the principle of competition as a dominant value, including other values such as ethics and compliance, which can be considered as an integration of a more general principle.

Ethics and *compliance* involve issues such as *accounting standards*, *criminal corporate liability* and *market abuse*. These are all issues where EU regulation has played a decisive role in forcing Member States' legislation to accept high standards of conduct after the corporate scandals that marked the beginning of the new century.

At the same time, "rules" imply **choices** and choices define the proper field of public regulatory law. As Nobel prize winner A. Sen states,

> *"when there are several objects of value, one alternative course of action may be more valued in one respect but less so in another"* and where there is room for *"plural evaluation, a clear overall ranking can, of course, be reached on the basis of 'dominance reasoning'"* [A. SEN (1987)].

Competition is a field that incorporates the prevalence of *dominant reasoning* whose implementation is entrusted to the antitrust institutions which are charged with a *single mission.*

A **dominant** value requires the competent authority to protect it *as such*. Policy implementation excludes the consideration of different interests. The absoluteness of "dominance reasoning" does not imply, in principle, any "balance" with other general principles, such as, in particular, industrial policy considerations (e.g. the creation of European industrial "champions").

The rationale of this domain goes back to the influence of the "ordoliberal vision":

> *"The ordoliberal vision presupposes a basic, binding commitment to a specific type of economic system, namely to a free market economy based on undistorted competition"* [A. HINAREJOS (2015)].

A dominant value requires specialized **institutions** with the power to enforce EU regulations to ensure impartial and uniform application of antitrust rules. Given the original (and rather persistent) national character of antitrust institutions, Member States are called upon to address common regulations and to give economic entities equal opportunity to compete and access the single market.

A single market in itself generates the need to *systematize the rules* that are fundamental to its functioning. Efficient enforcement of these rules fosters market development and creates a direct relationship between economic growth and rules. The close connection between the performance of economic activity and the proper behaviour that surrounds it is so strong that, in the event of failure to implement the rules, the market would be at risk. From this concept it follows that a **market** is considered **competitive**, on an **institutional basis**, when it has developed rules that are uniformly and consistently implemented.

Centralized and Shared Administration

EU rules on anti-competitive practices are characterized by the leading role of the EU Commission, apparently a case of centralized management recurring when

> *"EU legislation will impose obligations on the Commission to discharge policies without any systematic relationship with national administrations"* [P. CRAIG (2012)].

In the context of competition, however, the institutional pattern is more articulated.

On the one hand, the framework is based on the central role of the European Commission, as it has its own *competence:*

- on the exemption of agreements which do not have anti-competitive effects. The Commission provides for the individual agreements notified for *exemption*, but also establishes the policy of 'block exemptions' which authorizes broad types of agreements;
- on policies on *abuse of a dominant position*. A dominant position usually depends on a company's market share. Abuse is a generic term, but includes *refusal of supply*, *unfair prices* and *conditions*, *predatory pricing, loyalty rebates, exclusive obligations* and *abuse of intellectual property rights*.

On the other hand, the model works in a somewhat original approach compared to the paradigm of "central" and "shared" administration: the "shared" side consists of a "network" among the Member States' national antitrust authorities forming the *European Competition Network* (ECN). The network involves Member States' authorities in the decision-making process on the basis of certain criteria, essentially based on the size of the operation under consideration.

In the world of **contemporary global governance**, the model is not an exception. On the contrary:

> *"shared power is the rule. The overall picture is not hierarchical, because there are no multiple layers, in which fields are exclusive and interference between two areas does not exist* [...] *The two "levels" are not distinct, but are, rather, intertwined. States are not the only subjects, but combine with other subjects and thus lose their unity"* [S. CASSESE (2018)].

Therefore, in the context of EU governance, the ECN remains a vivid example of this general trend of the "*global legal space*", where there is a plethora of cases of *"composite decision-making"* or "network governance". The *European Competition Network* is obviously the proper implementation of such network governance that can be

> *"loosely defined as a set of relatively stable relationships of a non-hierarchical and interdependent nature linking a variety of actors, who share common policy goals"* [C. HARLOW, R. RAWLINGS (2014)].

An Institutional Network

The creation of a *network* of authorities derives from the need for uniformity among EU Member States.

In this respect, there was an institutional patchwork in the early 1990s.

Each Member State adopted – on the basis of EU competition rules (on monitoring agreements, abuse of dominant positions and mergers and acquisitions) – **different models** of **antitrust** institutions. This differentiated approach to the role, powers and relations of antitrust institutions with governments was the starting point of a *process of convergence* throughout the 1990s which achieved positive results in the early years of the new century.

Looking back, the models could be divided into three main categories: *quasi-jurisdictional*, *governmental* and *independent* authorities.

- In the first of the above models, the application of competition rules was entrusted to *quasi judicial bodies*. Thus in Spain the role of competition court was carried out by the *Tribunal de Defensa de la Competencia* which had the function of deciding and, in some cases, proposing competition issues. The Court was an autonomous body, but seconded to the Ministry of the Economy, which exercised efficiency control over its activity.
- In the "governmental" model (as was originally the case of the Netherlands), responsibility for the implementation of the Competition Act was entrusted to an authority operating under the Ministry of Economic Affairs, which excluded any kind of independence and autonomy.
- A mixed model was offered by the British experience in which the application of competition law was shared between "governmental" institutions and "independent" agencies (the *Monopolies and Mergers Commission* and the *Office of Fair Trading*), later replaced (since the *Enterprise and Regulatory Reform Act* 2013) by a classic *independent* model: the single-tier *Competition and Markets Authority* (CMA).

Differences between the supervisory policies and practices of the various *National Regulatory Authorities* (NRAs) led to *supervisory arbitrage* risk, a regulatory counterparty risk not allowed in an increasingly integrated European market. This was the reason for convergence, through various national reforms by Member States, and the adoption – as in the UK – of a **model** of absolute **independence** in all of them within the timeframe prescribed by economic orthodoxy.

Although uniformity is called for in this area, other external factors can still produce significant **distortions** in the **effective level playing field**: **taxation** above all. Significant differences in business taxation (due to fiscal dumping in countries – some of which are also founding Member States of the EU – such as Luxembourg and the Netherlands) present a

> *"highly diverse and fragmented picture throughout the various EU countries, which could create distortions and discriminations and, consequently, trigger opportunistic behavior both on the part of the Member States, providing low rates to encourage foreign businesses to set up shop, and of individual taxpayers, keen to exploit the favourable tax regimes"* [F. GALLO, in G. AMATO *et al.* (2019)].

In fact, while antitrust rules slightly reduced *law shopping* across the EU countries, they did not completely eliminate **competition** between **jurisdictions**. This is obviously a more globally relevant issue. The "*dark side*" of globalisation derives – among other things – from the asymmetry between – on the one hand – jurisdictions compliant with antitrust standards and state aid bans and – on the other – jurisdictions with limited or no regulation at all in these areas (China or Arabic countries compete worldwide through companies that are perfect "cartels" or monopolies).

However, even within the EU's super-regulated *legal order*, **"national identities"** are by no means excluded, e.g. an NRA that focuses the analysis of the "relevant market" on the national dimension of the market itself may limit a company's international growth.

Moreover, the manifold ways in which competition authorities in the EU consolidate the legal concept of the "relevant market" as an analytical tool of competition law, are currently under attack as a concept delineated in "static market environments". "Dynamic" and "innovation-driven markets" suggest the need for

> *"reconceptualising the legal framework for delineating antitrust markets in dynamic contexts"* in which *"companies frequently 'compete*

> *for a future market and not in an existing market'"* [V.H.S.E. ROBERTSON (2020)].

Contradictions are inevitable if the stated intention of the EU is to adopt a system based on the simultaneous application of the rules partly by the Commission and partly by the NRAs.

The inherent *contradiction* in the functioning of the *model* is mitigated by the fact that all national antitrust authorities work (or should work) closely together to ensure the enforcement of antitrust rules. The ECN is a stronghold for the enforcement of the EU system: it promotes closer cooperation between the Commission and NRAs in identifying the most appropriate authorities to investigate cross-border operations.

Perspectives on UK-EU Cross-border M&A Operations

M&A will be the most predictable *controversial sector* for cross mergers between UK and European companies.

The issue has long been debated between Member States and the EU itself. Some countries consider *merger policy* an important element of their *industrial policy* and not a concern of the Commission, provided that state aid and the rules on *"abuse of dominant position"* are respected.

The *European Control Merger Regulation* (ECMR) (Reg. n. 139/2004) is not a stand-alone regulation, but rather a pillar of **merger control** which also includes guidelines on the assessment of *horizontal mergers* and *best practices in merger investigations*. Under the regulation terms:

> *"A concentration which would significantly impede effective competition, in the common market or in a substantial part of it, in particular as a result of the creation or strengthening of a dominant position, shall be declared incompatible with the common market".*

The EU law on mergers and acquisitions with a cross-border dimension assumes that the EU is a *regional market.*

As a general rule, such mergers are normally reviewed at Commission level, in application of the "one-stop shop" concept and in compliance with the principle of subsidiarity.

Article 1(2) of ECMR establishes that a merger has a **community dimension** where:

> *"(a) the combined aggregate worldwide turnover of all the undertakings concerned is more than EUR 5000 million; and (b) the aggregate Community-wide turnover of each of at least two of the undertakings concerned is more than EUR 250 million, unless each of the undertakings concerned achieves more than two-thirds of its aggregate Community-wide turnover within one and the same Member State".*

Article 1(3) extends the attribution to the Commission for concentrations which do not *"meet the thresholds laid down in paragraph 2"* but have *"a Community dimension"* when specifically considered given quantitative figures are met.

In sum, EU legislation concerning the implementation of rules under Articles 101 and 102 TEU aims to facilitate and make more uniform the application of antitrust rules.

As a result, the issues of how to maintain a **level playing field** on **antitrust rules** were destined to be the bulk of the **negotiations** on the relationship between the UK and the EU after the transition period. The solution provided by the **Trade and Cooperation Agreement** can be accompanied by a reflection, recently launched at the EU level, on some *critical aspects* of EU *antitrust policy*.

A Franco-German Manifesto

The EU's strong commitment to the "dominant value" of competition led – in times of rapid change – to a conflict with other values such as the potential *growth of European industries* in a *globally competitive world*. **Criticism** of EU competition law is now shared by the leading Member States.

Since the Commission denied the Franco-German merger proposal of two large companies such as Alstom and Siemens [*European Commission Decision declaring a concentration to be incompatible with the internal market and the functioning of the EEA Agreement (Case M.8677 SIEMENS/ALSTOM)*, of 6 February 2019], which aimed to create a European champion in the **global space**, the dominant role of competition as a value in itself has now become contested.

Following the Commission's verdict, the two Member States issued the Franco-German Manifesto [*Bundesministerium für Wirtschaft und Energie, A* ***Franco-German Manifesto*** *for a European industrial policy fit for the 21st Century* (2019)] setting out the economic and political objectives for a "*genuine European industrial policy*", pooling the funding, skills and expertise of the two main drivers of the European economy.

Obviously, demoting the absoluteness of the "dominant value" principle when the EU's (or Member States') relevant interests are at stake in the global sphere implies *"adaptation"* of the *"regulatory framework"* to take into account *"industrial policy considerations"*.

Consequently, the **Franco-German Manifesto** states:

> *"We will only succeed if European companies are capable of competing on the global stage.*
> *Competition rules are essential but existing rules need to be revised to be able to adequately take into account industrial policy considerations in order to enable European companies to successfully compete on the world stage. Today, amongst the top 40 biggest companies in the world, only 5 are European.*
> *Despite our best efforts, which we must pursue, there is no regulatory global level playing field"* [*A Franco-German Manifesto* (2019)].

Given the resulting "massive disadvantage" deriving from the absence of a regulatory **global** level playing field, the issue is, on the one hand, to

> *"continue to argue for a fairer and more effective global level playing field, but in the meantime, we need to ensure our companies can actually grow and compete"* [*Ibid*].

The **Franco-German Manifesto** continues by proposing amendments to existing European competition rules. France and Germany suggest the option of:

> *"Updating current merger guidelines to take greater account of competition at the global level, potential future competition and the time frame when it comes to looking ahead to the development of competition to give the European Commission more flexibility when assessing relevant markets. This would enable a more dynamic and long-term approach to competition, at the global scale. This could entail adapting regulation no 139/2004 and current merger guidelines".*

Emergency *"Temporary Framework"* for "State Aid": Measures in the Pandemic Crisis

In the same vein *("taking greater account of competition at the global level")*, **state aid** is one of the central areas of concern. This concern derives from the perspective of looking at the UK as the next potentially divergent rival economy in a key area, as well as from the impact of the pandemic crisis on ordinary rules .

The Commission has the power to impose the *reimbursemen*t of *illegal state aid*, as defined in Articles 107 and 108 TFEU, according to which aid granted by the Member States, through public resources, in any form whatsoever which favours certain companies and types of production, distorts or threatens to distort competition, is incompatible with the single market (in the form of *grants*, *tax relief* or *state guarantees*).

Exemptions provided for in Article 107 (2) (3) TFEU) are aimed at *social policy*, or *underdeveloped areas*.

There is no difference – in state aid legislation – as to whether the favoured operator is a public or private entity.

The Commission, as guardian of the application of laws protecting competitiveness, applies the *market economy investor principle* in its assessment. According to this principle, aid may be granted to service providers that apply criteria of *economic return on investments similar* to those of a *company operating in the free market*.

In applying the rules to individual cases, the Commission takes into account the *macroeconomic context.* The key issue for the Commission is the *long-term viability* of the subsidies and whether the need for support stems from the *crisis* or a *specific emergency.*

In this context, the *governance package* for addressing the economic shock caused by the "pandemic crisis" included the Commission's decision to issue a *"Temporary Framework"* to soften state-aid rules in such a way as

> *"to expedite public support to companies, while ensuring the necessary level playing field in the Single Market"* [EU Council, *Report on the comprehensive economic policy response to the COVID-19 pandemic*, 9 April 2020].

Several communications were adopted by the Commission such as the *"Temporary Framework for State aid measures to support the econ-*

omy in the current COVID-19 outbreak" (20 March 2020, 2020/C 91 I/01), followed by a *Second*, (4 April 2020, 2020/C 112 I/01), *Third* (EU COM, 2 July 2020, 2020 C 218/03) and *Fourth Amendment* (EU COM, 13 October 2020). Accordingly, the above communications (collectively **Temporary Frameworks**) exempt Member States' intervention **from state aid regulations** until 30 June – 30 September 2021 (depending on the specific measures)

> *"to ensure liquidity and access to finance for undertakings* […] *in order to allow them to recover from the current situation"* [Amendment, I, sec. 1].

In this perspective, the application of EU state aid control must be *"targeted and proportionate"*. The communications identify specific state aid measures that the Commission considers compatible under Article 107(3) TFEU in light of the economic impact of the pandemic crisis. The list includes direct support to the economy (grants, loans, guarantees, export credit insurance, tax and advantages). The *Temporary Frameworks* are basically aimed at ensuring compatibility with EU legislation of short-term *incentives*.

Special attention is given to *"national public support in the form of equity and /or hybrid capital instruments to undertakings facing financial difficulties"* [EU COM, 8.5.2020, sec.7]. Initiatives at national level that aim to provide such support are identified by the Commission as a potential risk for a new wave of nationalism, or at least of an increase in public ownership.

Member States' initiatives – especially *"in strategic companies"* – are framed by the Commission within the general scheme of the neutral ownership principle (Article 345 TFEU), and as such allowed *"under conditions complying with the Market Economy Operator Principle"*.

The initiatives must be taken on a strictly temporary basis and must be based on *"proportionality"* not exceeding *"the minimum needed to ensure the viability of the beneficiary"*, providing for the state's *"appropriate remuneration for the investment"* (*"the closer the remuneration is to market terms, the lower the potential competition distortion caused by the State intervention"*). Safeguards in order to avoid distortions of competition include prohibiting beneficiaries from *"engag(ing) in aggressive commercial expansion financed by the State"* and devising an *"exit strategy for the State from the participation resulting from the recapitalisation"*.

> *"In this context, the Commission recalls that the TFEU is neutral as regards public versus private ownership (Article 345 TFEU). The conditions applicable to undertakings that are fully or partially State-owned to raise capital from public and private shareholders should be aligned with those applicable to private undertakings, whilst maintaining the same safeguards to preserve effective competition with the appropriate adjustments"* [EU COM, 2 July 2020].

A more significant long-term approach is planned in the adopted regulation *"as regards specific measures to provide exceptional flexibility for the use of the European Structural and Investments Funds"* still in response to the economic shock caused by the health crisis [*Regulation of the European Parliament and of the Council*, 20 April 2020, 2020/0054]. Flexibility is allowed in the implementation of the programmes supported by the *European Regional Development Fund* and the *Cohesion Fund*. *"With a view to alleviating the burden on public budgets responding to the public health crisis"* **cohesion policy** programmes will be totally supported by the above-mentioned funds without requiring co-financing from Member States. Provisions are also aimed at reducing "*administrative burdens"* when changes to the financial instruments are necessary.

"Towards open competition": the EU's Position and the UK's Approach

The UK's competition law was a permanent part of EU law and therefore – on exit day – had all the *key components* of the regulatory framework for *merger control*, *abuse of dominant position* and *anti-competitive agreement*, so as to prevent or mitigate adverse effects on competition.

> *"Since 1998 there has been a fundamental change in the structure and working of UK competition law from a public interest approach largely implemented by ministers to a competition-based approach implemented by independent authorities"* [T. PROSSER (2014)].

While there are significant differences between the corporate law systems of each EU Member State's domestic jurisdictions (as regards shareholder structure, access to finance, regulatory interventionism and litigation systems), the common adoption of "*best practices*" belonging to a modern and extensive framework of corporate law is essential for any *foreign direct investment* (as EU-UK cross-border operations are now to be considered).

This approach was already reflected in official UK documents preparing withdrawal from the EU: respect for the principle of competition was not presented in ritual form, but perceived as an *essential element* of the current form of the economy.

Thus, at that stage, the official positions of the United Kingdom, published in the **White Paper 2018** (*July 2018*), suggested agreement on

> "*binding provisions related to open and fair competition, with a common rulebook for state aid, cooperative arrangements on competition, and reciprocal commitments to maintain current high standards though non-regression provisions in other areas, such as environmental and employment rules*" (sec. 7).

The words imply the idea of continuing to control anti-competitive subsidies, as well as a robust state aid regime implemented by the CMA, a competition authority with significant powers and resources at its disposal to ensure open and fair competition.

Consequently, the already existing alignment with EU rules (largely forged with the Anglo-Saxon cultural contribution) should allow the CMA (former member of the ECN) to continue to work together with the EU Commission-DG Competition in order to manage parallel merger and antitrust investigations including provisions on the sharing of confidential information and co-operation on ongoing cases.

Similarly, the **Political Declaration**, which, as said, is a non-binding text, stated that

> "*the future relationship must ensure open and fair competition, encompassing robust commitments to ensure a level playing field.* [...] *These commitments should prevent distortions of trade and unfair competitive advantages. To that end, the Parties should uphold the common high standards applicable in the Union and the United Kingdom at the end of the transition period in the areas of state aid, competition, social and employment standards, environment, climate change, and relevant tax matters. The Parties should in particular maintain a robust and comprehensive framework for competition and state aid control*" (sec. 77).

On this basis – which is enhanced by geographical proximity and economic interdependence – the envisaged free trade agreement was supposed to include commitments to a **level playing field**, including adherence to "*the principles of good governance in the area of taxation and to the curbing of harmful tax practices*" (sec. 77).

However, there was *no legal obligation* to adopt such standards.

The wording was deliberately vague and non-committal. As already said (*supra* Ch. 1), it reflects the changes made after the previous draft of the *Withdrawal Agreement* had to be revised following the British Parliament's refusal to approve the text signed on 25 November 2018.

Without discussing here the specific difference between the two versions (only the last – signed on 17 October 2019 – is a legal text), it is sufficient to cite the *Explanatory Statement* by the *EU Parliament Committee on Constitutional Affairs* released on 23 January 2020:

> *"the changes to the text reflect the fundamental change of approach and level of ambition: references to the alignment of rules were removed from the parts of the text related to regulatory aspects, customs and checks and controls"* [...] *"As regards the level playing field, the text now refers to 'robust commitments to ensure a level playing field [which should] be commensurate with the scope and depth of the future relationship and the economic connectedness of the Parties'"*.

It follows – in the document's words – that the envisaged relationship:

> *"would require strong safeguards and level playing field provisions with a view to safeguarding the EU's internal market and avoiding placing EU firms at a potential unfair competitive disadvantage, and that any free trade agreement that fails to respect such levels of protection would not be ratified by Parliament"*.

This vision was strongly supported by the European institutions. The position of the EU Council was stated in its **Directives for the negotiation**, issued on 25 February 2020, for the future partnership in terms that:

> *"the United Kingdom should set up an independent and adequately resourced enforcement authority with effective powers to enforce the applicable rules, which should work in close cooperation with the Com-*

> *mission. Disputes about the application of State aid rules in the United Kingdom should be subject to dispute settlement"* [Directives for the Negotiation, sec. 15 (96)].

The position was articulated in normative terms in the **EU Draft Text** published on 18 March 2020, in which the *Commission Task Force* required that the *"effective enforcement"* of breach of rules *"which have as their object or effect the prevention, restriction or distortion of competition"* be ensured by the establishment or maintenance of *"an operationally independent authority"* (*"the relevant authority"*).

> *"The relevant authority shall have the necessary guarantees of independence from political or other external influence and shall be able to perform its duties and exercise its powers impartially"* [Part Two, Ch. Two, sec. 2].

This view was shared in principle by the **UK's Approach to negotiations** position paper, released on 27 February 2020, which states that the future partnership:

> *"should commit the parties to maintain effective competition laws, covering merger control, anticompetitive agreements and abuse of dominance"* [Part 1, sec. 66].

The position, however, adds that*"this does not require legal or regulatory alignment"* [*Ibid*]. The latter position has its own rationale in requiring that both parties have *"regulatory freedom to respond to new and emerging challenges in these areas"*.

The normative transposition of the position is given by the **UK Draft** Negotiating Document published on 19 May 2020 in terms confirming an overall definition of competition policy, aligned with the provisions of the Treaties:

> *"For the purposes of the Chapter:* [Chapter 22: Competition Policy] *"anti-competitive business conduct" means anti-competitive agreements between enterprises, concerted practices or decisions by associations of enterprises, anti-competitive practices by an enterprise that is dominant in a market, and mergers with substantial anti-competitive effects"* [Article 22.1].

At the same time, broad terms of reference recognize for the Parties *"the importance of free and undistorted competition in their trade relations"* and the commitment to take "*appropriate measures to proscribe anti-competitive business conduct*" referring to the prospect that:

> *"Their respective competition authorities shall endeavour to coordinate and cooperate in the enforcement of their respective competition law"* [Article 22.2].

In other words, the EU position required, in principle, continued *alignment* with EU principles, calling for high common standards to avoid a (feared) unfair competitive advantage of a competing economy.

The **UK's Approach** ruled out any recognition of alignment (or dynamic alignment to evolving EU competition rules), maintaining **regulatory freedom,** necessary to respond to – as quoted above – *"new and emerging challenges in this area"* .

The Relevant Competition Authority

As to the relevant authority in the UK legal system (i.e.the CMA), it is foreseen that it will actually be adequately resourced in terms of functions and relevant powers by the **UK Internal Market Act** (17 December 2020), Part 4 of which is wholly dedicated to *"Independent Advice on and Monitoring of UK Internal Market".*

The CMA's role is enhanced to include all the "*monitoring and reporting on the operation of the UK internal market*", playing an active role in undertaking "*a review of any matter it considers relevant to assessing or promoting the effective operation*" of the internal market (sec. 33).

Following the theme of "better regulation", widely theorized in the EU's mainstream thinking over the past few decades, the CMA retains the role of the "relevant authority" to evaluate the "*economic impact of a regulatory provision*" (sec. 36).

To adequately support the CMA for these functions, the authority will be endowed (sec. 32) with an **Office for the Internal Market** (OIM) with:

> *"the ability to provide independent, technical, non-binding expert advice to administrations on regulation or regulatory proposals that may impact the Internal Market".*

This is a reaffirmation of effective law enforcement power already noted in the **UK Internal Market White Paper**, where the point is proudly made:

> *"the UK is the only country in Europe whose competition authority can impose enforceable structural and behavioural remedies following a market investigation. These powers go beyond Regulation 1/2003, from which the EU derives its powers for a sectoral inquiry. The UK also has criminal sanctions for cartels and director disqualification powers which the European Commission and most Member States lack"* [**White Paper July 2020**, sec. 39].

Once again, intellectual foundations have nurtured legal concepts and language to which Anglo-Saxon and continental legal cultures have an important tribute to pay, too great to think that it can fade away under the (contingent) pressure of the present time.

Regulatory Freedom: Competition Law and State Aid in the *Trade and Cooperation Agreement*

However, the *fair share of compromises* during the negotiations – as honestly acknowledged in the UK's official **Summary** of the **Trade and Cooperation Agreement**, signed on 24 December 2020 – allowed the Parties to reach an agreed position on the issues raised, including the specific provisions on *"level playing field for open and fair competition and sustainable development"* (Part Two, Heading One, Title XI). They are part of a much broader regulatory framework developed by the TCA and are preceded (Title X) by provisions on *"good regulatory practices and regulatory cooperation"*. The constructive compromise reached is highlighted by the incipit (Title X) which recognizes *"regulatory freedom"*:

> *"Each Party shall be free to determine its approach to good regulatory practices under this Agreement in a manner consistent with its own legal framework, practice, procedures and fundamental principles"* (art. 1, sec. 1).

Coordination of regulatory measures, however, will be pursued through mechanisms involving a *Specialised Committee on Regulatory Cooperation* and *"publicly available descriptions of the processes"* used by each Party's regulatory authority *"to prepare, evaluate or review regulatory measures"*, as well as through *the "exchange of information on good regulatory practices"*. This is a broad framework of regulatory freedom highlighted by a declared willingness to co-operate.

The *"Title"* (Title X) on *Level Playing Field* is no less elusive as in its legal drafting.

The main lines of the solutions provided by the **TCA** can be recalled in a few key concepts:

- **accountability:** the Parties have a *"common understanding that their economic relationship can only deliver benefits in a mutually satisfactory way if the commitments relating to a level playing field for open and fair competition stand the test of time, by preventing distortions of trade or investment"*;
- **no harmonisation**: the *"Parties recognise that the purpose of this Title is not to harmonise the standards of the Parties";*
- **right to regulate**: the recognition of a claim to *"the right of each Party to set its policies and priorities (…), to determine the levels of protection it deems appropriate"*.

Even if placed in a framework of regulatory freedom for each Party, the specific provisions on **competition** and **state aid** appear quite aligned with the previous common regulatory framework.

Thus, with the intent to "square the circle", the provisions of the Title specifically dedicated to *"Competition policy"* sound like a confirmation of the "corpus" of competition rules shared in the years of membership:

> *"each Party shall maintain a competition law which effectively addresses the following anticompetitive business practices"*.

The provision goes on to list the "classic" issues of "agreements" and "*concerted practices*" that distort competition; "*abuse*" of "*a dominant position*"; (for the UK) "*mergers or acquisitions*" or (for the EU) *"concentrations*" that have significant anticompetitive effects.

The same can be said for the rules on *State Aid*. The relevant provisions (Title XI, art. 3) remain faithful to the definition already contained in the regulations applied in the UK during the membership period and then "**incorporated**" into the UK legal order by the **EUWA** (*European Union Withdrawal Act*), (*supra* Introduction).

The general approach is to ensure (at least in the immediate future) *continuity* in the application of rules that remain in force until they are repealed or amended by internal legislation.

The economic shock provoked by the **pandemic crisis**, however, allows *"exceptions"* referring to *"subsidies that are granted on a temporary basis to respond to a national or global economic emergency"*.

There is here a convergent approach with the aforementioned EU **Temporary Framework**, confirming that the *dynamic alignment* ruled out by the Agreement can still function under the pressure of new emerging challenges.

The development of a **joint regulatory framework** is to be expected not from abstract level playing field provisions– conditioned by the need for "identity" reaffirmations – but rather from **regulatory areas** (discussed here in the following Part 2): a landing zone that impinges more on operational functioning and less (much less) on *identitaire* issues.

Part 2

REGULATION

An Overview of the Scenario from 2021

Chapter 4
CONNECTING

"Roll up that map;
it will not be wanted these ten years"
(WILLIAM PITT, THE YOUNGER, 1806)

A Joint Regulatory Framework

The mythical sentence of William Pitt the Younger, pointing to the map of Europe: "it will not be wanted these ten years" proved wrong in 1806, taking almost ten years longer to establish the post-Napoleonic order. If we look at the ***map of European networks****, the above sentence would be equally wrong.*

Aside from the effect on competitive business strategy of any divergence of regulations, the unavoidable assumption is that markets are expanding geographically on the basis of physical or virtual interconnections that must be based on common principles. In this context, harmonisation, connection and infrastructure development are the best means to enable the physical movement of goods and people and to consolidate economic and social cohesion. These are the concepts inspiring the creation of ***Trans-European Networks*** *(TEN) which include "telecommunications, energy, transport and infrastructure" sectors.*

The ***Political Declaration*** *states in principle that the parties will maintain regulatory autonomy. At the same time (and in the same section) it recognizes that future provisions should establish common principles in "the fields of standardisation, technical regulations" (sec. 23).*

The reason is not merely the expectation of avoiding unnecessary barriers, but rather a ***technological necessity*** *for uniformity of rules to ensure* ***interconnections*** *among networks.*

Rules *– such as those that regulate markets – constitute* ***goods*** *in an* *economic sense, and therefore an investment, since their functioning is essential for the community, beyond the usefulness of calculation.*

As Nobel prize winner J. E. Stiglitz pointed out in his latest book:

> *"We take a broad perspective on rules. In our usage, the word includes a panoply of institutions and regulations, both formal and explicit as well as informal and implicit. While markets are important, even the best-performing markets cannot solve many of society's key problems. There is an important societal role for the public sector (government) and for civil society"* [J.E. STIGLITZ (2020)].

It is "substantive rationality" – even more than a common platform of ideas – that requires a ***joint regulatory framework****. While formal rationality imposes conditions for the legitimacy of the process, substantive rationality has obvious conceptual and relevant implications: rationality is "substantive when it governs the actual outcome of distributive decisions" [R.M. UNGER (1976)].*

Utilities*, as well as* ***networks*** *and* ***infrastructure****, constitute the core of the societal role played by the public sector and their development is an essential part of a society's distribution decisions.*

The point is not weakened by "light-tough regulation", in proper British "style". Common law foundations provide grounds for principles bound by rules:

> *"the virtue of common law is said to be its capacity to develop from bottom up to deal with the world as it is rather than as we would wish it to be, to respond to social change in a cautious but effective manner"* [D.J. GALLIGAN (2007)].

The old saying that "corporations have neither bodies to be punished, nor souls to be condemned" has long since been overtaken by ***legal regulatory frameworks****. These concern the ways in which a nation state (or, like the EU, a supranational state, better equipped on technical issues than the nation state) can cope with the power of companies, especially when they work on* ***connecting*** *public* ***utilities*** *or natural monopolies such as* ***networks*** *or act as counterparties in* ***contracting*** *infrastructure (infra Ch. 5) or require* ***equivalence*** *in the management of financial services (infra Ch. 6); in other words, when* ***public goods*** *are at stake.*

Regulating Networks

It was the utilities sector that in the nineties experienced an *accelera-tion spectaculaire* in terms of technical and regulatory development. The "roaring nineties" are now considered in contemporary literature as a period of a new "merchant" order or a new "supercapitalism", the projection of an ideal market in which the role of the legislator had to be limited to defining "property rights".

In fact, the pendulum between market and institutions had already begun to swing from the repudiation of market fundamentalism towards an appropriate balance between government and market that needs government intervention, but not intervention that would frustrate market solutions.

> *"It's worth recalling that all great promoters of the market economy, including Adam Smith, John Maynard Keynes, Paul Samuelson, Friedrich Hayek, and Milton Friedman, were fully aware of the reality or public goods, environmental spillovers, and asymmetric information"* [...] *"In summary, the markets themselves require interventional public function for distribution, production or provision of public goods"* [J. SACHS (2011)].

The legal analysis supports the economic approach to **regulation** with specific reference to legislative intervention:

> *"The events of recent years have shown that governments have been called on to intervene in ways which are far deeper, and far more costly, than merely setting a framework of regulation. Moreover, the range of techniques used is much wider than the use of conventional regulatory instruments"* [T. PROSSER (2014)].

The balance between market and institutions requires continuous adjustment in the form of specific regulations which – from time to time – mark the possible balance of interests in the areas of public goods such as in the **telecommunications**, **energy** or **transport** sectors. Balancing the interests in the various sectors leads to the need for control by assigning regulatory tasks to a specific "authority" in order to manage "information asymmetries". In some cases, regulation represents a "substitute" for competition, due to inadequate market conditions or insufficient liberalisation of specific sectors.

Justifications for public regulation are given by well-known assumptions:

> *"Regulation is driven by different motives, some based on efficiency and practicality, others on values such as fairness, non-discrimination, and a sound environment"*. At the same time *"the clamor of fractions and the power of special interests can also be the motivation"* [D.J. GALLIGAN (2007)].

In other words, the economic game does not ensure that the distributive policies emerging from the competitive process are in accordance with the prevailing concept of equity, and, in any case, the economy may not be perfectly competitive.

Moreover, even if the economy reflects the competitive equilibrium model, the outcome may not be efficient because of *externalities*.

Market discipline gives rise to a plurality of solutions that have an impact on the organization of the market and can be conceived as *methods to balance values* and *resolve conflicts* which are, to a certain extent, "endemic" to any contemporary society. Through *regulatory mechanisms* or through *distributive policy decisions*, markets of public goods, e.g. goods consisting of *networks, services* and *infrastructure,* are defined and regulated by public authorities. It is in such markets – more than elsewhere – that private autonomy would not automatically result in "economic freedom" in the market if there were no "adjustment". The rules themselves reflect the state of evolution of the *value conflict* between *social needs* and *economic requirements*. This reconciliation requires a balance in terms of regulatory discipline.

This is an argument that on a more theoretical level has given rise to a debate on the erosion of the idea of legality based on formal rational authority in favour of pervasive **substantial rationality**. It is a concept that emerges from the limits of a legal system based on the formulation and application of general rules in the face of the *"complexity and variability of the situations sought to be regulated"* [D.J. GALLIGAN (1986)].

The Original Framework

Recognition of the regulatory framework provided for by the **Trade and Cooperation Agreement** should start with a brief recap of the framework shared on exit day by both Parties of the *new partnership*.

A technical regulatory characteristic is that all utilities are based on the concept of *network*. The notion can be captured in a dynamic dimension. The network is used for public service purposes: whatever the regime of ownership is (whether public or private), the network is a **public good** because it is used for public service. The emphasis here shifts from legal *property status* to the *economic function* of the asset.

The "public powers" approach in the area of "public goods" involves several issues. The two EU "pillars" involved are an **economic** one based on "*market economy*" and a **social** pillar based on the concept of "*social cohesion*". The **balance** of these two primary **values** implies la *"recherche d'un équilibre entre différents impératifs publics"* [M. LOMBARD, in M. FREEDLAND *et al.* (2006)] and determines the legal framework (rules and institutions) for the governance of the public goods market in Europe today.

The EU considers the development of networks essential to achieving the dual objectives of a fully integrated internal market and the strengthening of "*economic, social and territorial cohesion*".

The main purpose of regulation in this respect is therefore to allow competition to develop while protecting public and consumer interests. The Treaties provide the definition of the functioning of the networks:

> *"within the framework of a system of open and competitive markets, action by the Union shall aim at promoting the interconnection and interoperability of national networks as well as access to such networks"* [Article 170 TFEU (2)].

The balance between social cohesion (considered essential for the European *model of civilization*) and competitive markets inspires the creation of *services of general interest* (SGI) that must be able to guarantee *universal access*, i.e., the obligation to supply a certain *service* throughout the *national territory* at an *affordable price* and at the same *level of quality* in remote places and urban areas in difficulty.

The basic SGI criteria are to ensure *equitable access, safety of performance and continuity of service*, as well as quality and public control and liability for performance of the service.

Member States have a wide margin of discretionary power in deciding whether and how to implement the supply of services of general interest.

The basic concept is that services of general interest are seen as an essential factor in the European **model of society**. Article 106 (2) TFEU confirms that such a concept is part of the Union's **common values framework** and acknowledges its role in promoting social and territorial cohesion. This approach is in itself a version of the EU's economic constitution, incorporating

> *"a deliberately designed set of principles to promote a particular value or set of social values",* [which includes] *"not only economic freedom and efficiency but also social and redistributive values"* [T. PROSSER (2014)].

At the same time, Member States may choose the financing mechanism to be applied. Generally, Member States are required to adopt all necessary measures to achieve the objectives of economic and social cohesion, environmental protection and supply safety. Such measures may also include the provision of economic **incentives**.

Member States are required to notify the Commission of all measures taken to fulfil **universal service** and **public service obligations** and to protect consumers and the environment, as well as any other measure that may affect national and international competitiveness. The Commission must be informed every two years of any changes to these measures.

The main limitation to this discretionary power is that the financing mechanism must not create distortions of competitiveness in the single market.

In fact, EU legislation does not treat the SGI in a particularly favourable way, excluding cases in which their general interest mission would be undermined.

The non-competitive effects are justified only if they occur in the pursuit of the general interest. From this point of view, the concept of "service of general interest" does not justify a privileged position, not only in terms of entrustment of the service, but also from a financial and fiscal point of view.

Disentangling Networks

On exit day the approach summarized above was part of the Common Regulatory Framework.

The **UK's Approach to negotiations** had already made it clear that in the future relationship the Parties would agree on the commitment that:

> *"State Owned Enterprises operate in a fair and transparent manner and do not discriminate against businesses"* [Part 1, sec. 69].

The statement is directed to

> *"enterprises where the state has significant control through full, majority, or minority ownership"* [but] *"should cover designated monopolies and any enterprise granted special rights or privileges by the State"* [Part 1, sec. 70].

From the current perspective, some economic sectors are directly interested in the Common Regulatory Framework:

> *"There are three UK-wide network industries and associated services which interact extensively with the EU: transport, energy and communications. All three are important in their own right and are key 'enablers' to the functioning and success of the economy as a whole"* [UK Gov. (2016)].

The above statement – albeit contained in a document dating back to the process leading up to exit day – describes as **key-enablers** those economic services sectors where a joint regulatory framework is inevitable on **technical** rather than legal grounds.

The **Political Declaration** recognized this point by stating that

> *"the period of the United Kingdom's membership of the Union has resulted in a high level of integration between the Union's and the United Kingdom's economies* [...] *The future relationship will inevitably need to take account of this unique context"* (sec. 5).

On the basis of these assumptions, the document went on to state that regulation should include

> *"specific regulatory provisions in sectors of mutual interest such as telecommunication services, financial services"* adopting *"domestic regulation that reflects good regulatory practices"* (sec. 32).

The regulation of utilities has long been recognized as an emerging field of the *"complexity of policy networks which are now characteristic of modern governance"* [P. LEYLAND, in N. BAMFORTH *et al.* (2003)]. Issues such as the various methods of **accountability**, the need for multi-layered **commitment** and implications for **institutional design** are evidence of this complexity.

Some assumptions are central: as the **Political Declaration** recognizes

> *"the sizes of the two economies and their geographic proximity* [...] *have led to complex and integrated supply chains"* (sec. 16).

For these reasons, the utilities area is one where the expectation of greater **flexibility** must be harmonized with **technical challenges** due to the state of integration of *virtual* and *physical networks.*

Market Governance

As a preliminary and general point, it must be considered that – at the EU level – all utilities sectors are gradually progressing towards **EU single markets**: the process is particularly advanced in the telecommunication, energy, air and rail transport sectors. However, the main institutional role is still played by *National Regulatory Authorities* (NRAs).

These NRA must be independent and have the task of ensuring real competitiveness, non-discrimination, and effective market financing on the basis of the guidelines laid down in the EU regulation.

The rules state that NRAs must pursue their objectives taking into account general *policy guidelines* formulated by the government. To some extent, these provisions limit the scope of the tasks assigned to the NRAs, excluding the authorities from defining their own political guidelines.

This result, which theoretically affects the NRAs' independence and autonomy of judgment and evaluation, is however balanced by another set of powers conferred on the Authorities:

- powers to submit *proposals* to the government and parliament regarding the services that are subject to concession or authorisation and renewal, as well as to any change to the single act of concession;
- formal and substantial *regulatory power*, both general and specific, on the technical-economic conditions of access and interconnection to the network and the tariffs and quality of service levels;
- *control functions*, linked to the operation of the market as a whole, in particular as regards access to services and the application of service charters;
- *powers to sanction* any breach of service suppliers' obligations to public authorities or users.

To properly assess conformity, the authorities use the provisions of contracts stipulated with governments, service regulations and general conditions of service providers.

The regulatory framework for public utility services is often completed by a multi-year *"contract du plan"* (the French experience being the leading case) to be concluded, unless otherwise provided by law, between the government and the service supplier as an ordinary instrument to regulate the services in question, including investment, tariffs and quality.

In this regulatory context, NRAs work to improve *efficiency* and *value for money* in supplying services, as a method of ensuring particularly important control where

> *"a delicate balance has to be struck between public (political) and private (market) forms of accountability"* [P. CANE, in J. EEKELAAR, J. BELL (1987)].

Although the dominant role belongs to the national regulatory authorities, for the telecommunications and energy markets, the need for coordination has given rise to European *network governance* composed of EU supervisory authorities, such as respectively the *Body of European Regulators for Electronic Communications* (BEREC) and the *Agency for the Cooperation of Energy Regulators* (ACER).

In the sectors of public utilities, supranational institutions are less authoritative and have more an advisory role: this is the case for the BEREC and the ACER.

"It is predicated on the fact that both EU and national administration have related but distinct tasks for the delivery of the regulatory objectives, which are commonly set out in legal terms in the enabling legislation. Regulatory policy in areas as diverse as agriculture, the Structural Funds, financial regulation, telecommunications and utilities regulation is run in this manner" [P. CRAIG (2015)].

All the sectors, however, engender *shared competences,* considering the dominant role of EU legislation (mainly through directives) and the competing role of national legislation (each with its own national regulatory authority).

Public Goods

It has been clear from the beginning of the negotiations that the effectiveness of the new partnership will largely depend on the principles that guide the regulatory approach.

The EU Council **Directives for negotiation** stated the point (from the EU side):

"While preserving the regulatory autonomy of the Parties, the envisaged partnership should include provisions to promote regulatory approaches that are transparent, efficient, and compatible to the extent possible" (sec. 38).

The quality, efficiency and proper dissemination of services throughout the national territory are, as mentioned above, included in the general aims of the regulation.

Consequently,

"the envisaged partnership should include cross-cutting disciplines on good regulatory practices and transparency for the development and implementation of efficient, cost-effective regulations for services and investment" (sec. 42).

Any approach to the "partnership" in the utilities sector needs to be articulated *from market to market*, depending on the characteristics of the network.

On this basis, the analysis undertaken below addresses:

a) *liberalised markets* where the *network* (privately or publicly owned) is surrounded by public "guarantees" regarding its use in terms of accessibility by suppliers. One case is given by the **telecommunications** market;
b) *conformed markets*, when the "separation" of the market into "segments" of production (e.g. *"up-stream"*, *"mid-stream"*, *"down-stream"* for **electricity or gas**) creates a special regulatory system for each market segment. The market is "conformed" in the sense that the market itself is *defined by regulation*. It is regulation that allows entities to operate and institutions to play a role in the functioning of the markets;
c) *reserved markets* where the network is managed by an economic operator, to which the network is allocated to ensure universal service as is the case of rail **transport**.

a) Liberalised Market: the *Electronic Communication Framework*

The first directives for the liberalisation of this sector were adopted in the 1990s. The most recent EU directives present some innovations in three key areas:

- the transition from the initial process of liberalisation to the more mature phase where the principle of *separation between infrastructure and services* lays the basis for allowing users of one company to access services offered by another company (interconnection) when there are several networks. In this context, importance is also given to issues such as the access "price" (which cannot act as a "barrier" to market entry) or "denial" of access;
- the definition of a *unified legal framework* for the entire electronic communications sector, including telecommunications, radio-TV and new information technologies, with the prospect of *technological convergences* among the various media. The process of convergence of services and networks has been accelerated by digital technology. The concept of *technological neutrality* aims to avoid the situation in which the same content (be it information, images or digital data) is subject to different regulatory treatment solely because it is provided by different platforms;
- the definition of a *platform of rules* for national regulatory au-

thorities, including plans to strengthen relations between the authorities of the various EU countries as well as between regulatory and antitrust authorities and the European Commission.

As already mentioned, the clear need for **technical interconnection** in **communications services** has been stated by the UK since the beginning of exit negotiations:

> *"With respect to communications networks, telecoms operators are regulated in the UK by the EU's 'Electronic Communications Framework', which promotes competition and choice. As we exit the EU, we will want to ensure that UK telecoms companies can continue to trade as freely and competitively as possible with the EU and let European companies do the same in the UK"* [**White Paper** (2017)].

These were the same concepts that inspired the European Union to recognize the importance of creating *Trans-European Networks*, pursuing the dual objective of integrating the internal market and strengthening **economic**, **social** and **territorial cohesion.**

The point is restated by the Parties in the **Political Declaration**:

> *"The Parties should provide, through sectoral provisions in telecommunication services, for fair and equal access to public telecommunication networks and services to each other's services suppliers and address anticompetitive practices"* (sec. 39).

The above sentence is reproduced almost literally in the EU Council's **Directives for negotiation** (sec.40) and in the **UK's Approach to negotiations** [Part 1, sec. 50].

The **EU Draft Text** – issued by the *Commission Task Force* for negotiations – provided, to this end, regulatory definitions of the basic common concepts of *"essential facilities"*, *"interconnection"*, *"network element"*, *and "universal service"*, i.e. *"the minimum set of services of specified quality that must be made available to all users"* [Part II, Title VI, Ch. V, sec. 4].

On the other side, the **UK Draft**, while aligned in the relevant definitions, focused attention on the fact that:

> *"Each Party shall ensure that its telecommunications regulatory body is legally distinct from, and functionally independent to any supplier of*

> *public telecommunications networks, equipment and services"* [Chapter 14, Article 14.3].

The view on *"independence and impartiality"* of regulatory bodies is the premise for setting out the principle that:

> *"Each Party shall endeavour to authorise the provision of telecommunications networks or services without a formal procedure and permitting the supplier to start providing its networks or services upon simple notification"* [Article 14.4].

Although various measures may be *"necessary to ensure the security and confidentiality of communications"*, access to *"essential facilities"* would be considered a *"right"* with the related *"obligation to negotiate interconnection"*.
The **TCA**, in the chapter on "**Regulatory Framework**" (Part 2, Heading One, Title II, *Services and Investment*) includes "*Telecommunications Services*" (Section 4). EU values such as "*Universal Service*" are safeguarded by preventing universal service providers from engaging "*in market distortive practices*". Regulatory freedom implies however each Party's right "*to define the kind of universal service obligation it wishes to maintain*".
In this context, the full range of notions elaborated in EU regulatory activity are retained as part of a shared language (e.g. for "*essential facilities*", "*interconnection*", "*network element*"). Therefore each **regulatory authority** in the sector will be *"legally distinct and functionally independent"* and "*impartial with respect to all market participants*".
The **TCA** confirms the conceptual construction developed during the membership period, such as the rights to *access* and *use telecommunications networks.* The *"obligation to negotiate interconnection for the purposes of providing public telecommunications networks or public telecommunications services"* implies a "clause" of "**non – regression**" with regard to the existing level of liberalisation.

b) Conformed Markets: the IEM (*Internal Energy Market*) and Energy Trading under TCA rules

The current state of the energy market can be seen as a paradigm of a market "segmented" by the regulatory process. As already mentioned, the sector is structured on three levels: power generation (*upstream*), long-distance transmission (*midstream*) and local distribution (*downstream*). For each of these segments, the EU regulation determines the actors and activities involved, so that there are different regulatory disciplines for *generation*, *transmission* and *distribution*.

The process of *segmentation of markets* started at the beginning of the liberalisation process through the provision on *unbundling* of the transmission network on the one hand and generation and distribution on the other. The measure was considered essential to ensure that the network operator maintains the profile of *disinterest* and *independence* necessary for electricity and gas markets to operate under competitive conditions.

In particular, EU Directives require Member States to ensure that "midstream" operators are separate legal entities other than energy production or distribution operators. The aim is to ensure the independence of the network operator from the interests of the "upstream" and "downstream" operating industries.

Network infrastructure is thus conceived as an **essential facility**: infrastructure is open to all operators (with all the resulting obligations for the owner to guarantee its use to third parties as well). The "neutral ownership" principle allows ownership of the network to be transferred from public to private, provided that compliance with obligations imposed by the regulatory authority is respected.

On this basis, the Union's energy policy shall aim to:

> "*a) ensure the functioning of the energy market; b) ensure security of energy supply in the Union; c) promote energy efficiency and energy saving and the development of new and renewable forms of energy; and d) promote the interconnection of energy networks*" [Article 194 TFEU].

The above indicated objectives

> "*shall not affect a Member State's right to determine the conditions for exploiting its energy resources, its choice between different energy sources and the general structure of its energy supply*" [*Ibid*].

Technical aspects are central in this area and aimed at ensuring that the interconnections of the Member States' networks give rise to an **Internal Energy Market** (IEM).

As has been seen for the communications sector, the technical need for interconnection is widely recognised in the UK's official statements, even in the energy market:

> *"With respect to energy, EU legislation underpins the coordinated trading of gas and electricity through existing interconnectors with Member State, including Ireland, France, Belgium and the Netherlands. There are also plans for further electricity interconnections between the UK and EU Member States and EEA Members. These coordinated energy trading arrangements help to ensure lower prices and improved security of supply for both the UK and EU Member States by improving the efficiency and reliability of interconnector flows, reducing the need for domestic back-up power and helping balance power flows as we increase the level of intermittent renewable electricity generation"* [**White Paper** (2017)].

Following these statements, the **White Paper 2018** *(July 2018)* reinforced the idea of a *common rulebook* in this area:

> *"The UK wants to explore with the EU the option for the future energy relationship.*
> *One option would be for the UK to leave the Internal Energy Market (IEM). In this case, the UK would explore what would be needed to ensure trade over interconnectors would continue without automatic capacity allocation via the IEM system. An alternative option would be for the UK to participate in the IEM to preserve the existing efficient trading practices over interconnectors. In this case, the UK would need a common rulebook with the EU on the technical rules for electricity trading".*

Following these previous positions, the **Political Declaration** added a general vow to establish

> *"a framework to facilitate technical cooperation between electricity and gas networks operators and organizations, such as the European Networks of Transmission System Operators for Electricity and Gas, in the planning and use of energy infrastructure connecting their systems. The framework should also include mechanisms to ensure as far as possible security of supply and efficient trade over interconnectors over different timeframes"* (sec. 65).

As can be seen, the crucial issue of regulatory alignment actually depends on unavoidable technical aspects, moving – in this case – from an EU regulation that has assumed the characteristics of *standards* for *connecting different infrastructure*.

In a wider perspective the EU **Directives for negotiation** affirmed the expectation to

> *"explore the possibility of setting transparent and non-discriminatory rules for exploration and production, and specific market access rules and include provisions on renewable energies"* (sec. 79).

On the other hand, the **UK's Approach to negotiations** restated the point that an agreement on energy must reflect its interests and that *"the UK will make independent decisions on its energy policies"* [Part 2, sec. 9], an "approach" that suggests a more limited basic arrangement based on an undefined appeal to "*independent decisions*" on "*energy policies*".

Building on these widely shared conceptual and technical constructs, it is no coincidence that "*Energy*" gives rise, in the **TCA** (under Title VIII, Part 2), to intense perspectives of trade and cooperation.

Provisions include *trading electricity* and *gas* through *interconnectors*, integrating *renewables* and cooperation to develop and implement trading arrangements by April 2022. The technical prerequisite for a future arrangement is a joint commitment to integrate renewable and other *clean technologies* in line with the zero net emissions goal.

Once again, the transition from the *Internal Market* to the *distinct legal orders* takes place in this area within a **joint regulatory framework**, removing unnecessary barriers to trade.

c) The Civil Nuclear Sector and the *Nuclear Cooperation Agreement*

Independence in energy policy basically refers instead to the **civil nuclear sector**. Throughout the entire period of UK membership this area was regulated by the *European Atomic Energy Community* (EURATOM). Withdrawal from the EU affected the agreement in the sectors because it included withdrawal from Euratom, a separate legal entity but governed by EU institutions.

The theme outlined in the **UK's Approach to negotiations** clearly indicated regulation of nuclear energy as one of the most important issues to resolve. The sector includes arrangements in such sensitive areas as *nuclear safeguards* and *trade* in *nuclear materials*:

"The Euratom Treaty provides the legal framework for civil nuclear power generation and radioactive waste management for members of the Euratom Community, all of whom are EU Member States. This includes arrangements for nuclear safeguards, safety and the movement and trade of nuclear materials both between Euratom Members such as France and the UK, as well as between Euratom Members and third countries such as the US" [**White Paper** (2017)].

Once Euratom was included in the withdrawal, the official position was better defined in a subsequent document with a view to multi-level cooperation, aiming to:

"establish a cooperation mechanism between the UK safeguards regulator (the Office for Nuclear Regulation) and Euratom, enabling activity such as technical information exchanges, joint studies and consultation on regulatory or legislative changes;
ensure continuity of contractual arrangements for the supply of nuclear material [...];
minimize barriers and simplify export control arrangements in the trade and transfer of sensitive nuclear materials, equipment and technology between the UK and the Euratom Community" [**White Paper** 2018 (*July 2018*)].

In a forward-looking scenario, the means to co-operate on nuclear issues was a matter for negotiation, as an issue of important priority for the nuclear industry and of strategic importance for the parties. The framework for this envisaged cooperation needed to be established – as far as legal terms are concerned – within the framework of international collaboration on nuclear research and development.

The **Political Declaration** confirmed the "*importance*" – in the context of the future relationship – of cooperation between Euratom and the UK regulator as a matter of international law:

"This should include exchange of information in areas of mutual interest such as safeguards, safety and cooperation with the International Atomic Energy Agency (IAEA)" (sec. 66).

The intention of the Parties was clearly reaffirmed by the UK's position which envisaged a *nuclear cooperation agreement* that *"should facilitate civil nuclear trade while maintaining the parties' commitments to non-proliferation"* [**UK's Approach to negotiations**, part 2, sec. 25]. Specific contents on safeguards, technical issues and sharing co-operation were also detailed.

Likewise, the EU Council aimed at *"wide ranging co-operation"* in the sector

> *"underpinned by commitments to maintaining the highest possible standards of nuclear safety and radiation protection applying at the end of the transition period"* (**Directives for negotiation**, sec. 84).

The above declared intentions were confirmed in a full-fledged **international treaty** in this area, signed on the same date (24 December 2020).

The **Nuclear Cooperation Agreement** (**NCA**) is separate from the **TCA** being signed by the UK and EURATOM.

The **NCA** provides for broad cooperation on all relevant civil nuclear issues, including *safeguards*, *safety* and *security*, as required for Parties fully responsible in civil nuclear practices (including nuclear weapons non-proliferation).

d) Reserved Markets: the *European Common Aviation Area*

The principles of *interconnection, interoperability* and *access* to networks are common to all utility markets and, as seen above, are now essential elements of the common regulatory framework devised by the **TCA**.

With regard to the distinction between *liberalised*, *conformed* and *reserved markets,* the paradigm of reserved market applies to the *transport sectors* Here, the operation requires the granting of special rights in favour of companies allowed to operate in the sectors. Physical networks are always subject to the *right of equitable and non-discriminatory access*, opening up the business to *non-national carriers* as well.

As in the other utilities sectors, the technicality and complexity of disentangling the overall networks in the sector was perfectly recognised by the official UK positions:

> *"In the transport sector, there is a substantial body of EU law covering four transport modes (aviation, roads, rail and maritime), which governs our current relationship with the EU, and which will need to be taken into consideration as we negotiate our future relationship"* [**White Paper** (2017)].

The **Political Declaration** on the point was rather general:

> *"The Parties agree that bilateral arrangements should be established, as appropriate, for cross-border rail services, including to facilitate the continued smooth functioning and operation of rail services"* (sec. 61).

The objectives were better indicated in relation to the *European Common Aviation Area*. In this respect, the ***Political Declaration*** stated the aim of the Parties – within the framework of the future relationship – to reach a

> *"Comprehensive Air Transport Agreement"* that *"should cover market access and investment, aviation safety and security, air traffic management, and provisions to ensure open and fair competition"* (sec. 58).

The (previously) common regulations on air transport make the sector the most open to competition in the transport area.

In the 1990s, the EU defined the modalities of access to routes and public service.

In short, the programme for liberalising the sector focussed on two main issues:

- determining the economic actors entitled to carry out air transport (with an international license valid for all operators);
- liberalising tariff systems and secondary activities (e.g. handling services).

Over the course of two decades, there has been a shift from bilateral agreements based on international conventions with public companies belonging to the individual EU Member States (the so-called national airlines) to a system of **global cooperation** among all the players with substantial market power.

As in the other utilities sector, the related UK documents are crystal clear in recognising the parties' interest in reaching arrangements to maintain and develop **connectivity:**

> *"In the late 1980s and early 1990s the EU created an internal aviation market whereby any carrier licensed in the EU is entitled to operate any service in the EU, superseding the old bilateral arrangements. As we exit the EU, there will be a clear interest for all sides to seek arrangements that continue to support affordable and accessible air*

> *transport for all European citizens, as well as maintaining and developing connectivity"* [**White Paper** (2017)].

A further document states from the industry point of view that:

> *"The UK has the largest aviation industry in Europe, and the UK's geographical position in the network is key, with around 80 per cent of all North Atlantic traffic passing through UK or Irish controlled airspace"* [**White Paper** 2018 (*July 2018*)].

Accordingly, the aim was*:*

> "[to] *explore options for maintaining reciprocal liberalized access through an Air Transport Agreement. This would permit UK and EU carriers to operate air services to, from and within the territory of both the UK and the EU on an equal basis. This could be supported through an approach to ownership and control that avoids introducing additional barriers to businesses"*. [*Ibid*]

The above point (*"approach to ownership and control"*) was actually crucial, since by leaving the EU's single aviation market, British airline companies would – as a result – lose the operating rights that come with it.

The **UK's Approach to negotiations** was quite precise in defining the terms of a *Comprehensive Air Transport Agreement* with regard to the objectives (a *"liberalized market access for air services on a reciprocal basis"* and *"interoperability between UK and EU airspace"*), the contents (**traffic rights** for the parties' companies to operate *"without restrictions on frequency or capacity"*); **ownership** (*"no unnecessary restrictions on the nationality"*); **modern commercial practices** (*"with minimal administrative burden"*) and the **technical aspects** as to *"aviation security and air traffic management (avoiding trade distortions through appropriate governance arrangements)* [*UK's Approach to negotiations* (2020), Part 2, sec. 6-7]

The EU Council's **Directives for negotiation** raised the issue in more general terms:

> *"The envisaged partnership should address comprehensively the aviation relationship with the United Kingdom and consider arrangements typically included in Union bilateral aviation agreements. It should ensure, on the basis of commercial principles and fair and equal opportunities to compete, a reciprocal, sustainable and balanced opening of*

markets while preserving the internal market for air transport services" (sec. 61).

As for other sectors, the principles elaborated in the context of the previous single legal order are confirmed by the **TCA** in the specific rules (Part 2, Heading Two – *Aviation*) covering arrangements for the operation of air transport services between the UK and the EU. These rules allow ample space for cooperation and consultation commitments in the field of air traffic management, aviation security and consumer protection.

In the scenario summarized above, looking at the different utility network sectors, it is clear that each area required *sectorial regulatory disciplines*, identifying the key factors and the *cross-cutting issues*.

A **strategic** approach was needed to determine the extent to which this opportunity could be exploited.

The recovery of **regulatory sovereignty** will certainly imply some divergence from EU rules. On the other hand, the regulatory approach in the utility area – where the EU has unparalleled regulatory capacity – will require **compliance with technical standards** to maintain the advantage of (and the need for) *interconnections* and *connectivity* with *European-wide networks*, without quantitative restrictions and operational flexibility in light of mutual economic benefits. **Utilities** is an area where the single legal order has produced terminology, as well as conceptual and practical approaches, now inevitably shared by the two new distinct legal orders, somewhat compelling **separate markets** to result in a **joint regulatory framework** that pursues mutual economic benefits.

Chapter 5
CONTRACTING

"I ask Hon Members to note the word 'economic'. The Treaty of Rome does not deal with defence. It does not deal with foreign policy. It deals with trade and some of the social aspects of human life which are most connected with trade and production"
(H. MACMILLAN, addressing the House of Commons 1961)

Procurement Market and Private Litigation Framework

The words pronounced by then Prime Minister Harold Macmillan at the Parliament at Westminster on 2 August 1961 (HC Deb vol. 645 c 1481), asking for the House's support for approval of the "application" to join the (then) European Economic Community (which France subsequently vetoed), designated ***economic competence*** *as the EEC's exclusive area of interest.*

Reference was made to "trade and production" (regulatory framework), i.e. "aspects of human life", which remained at the core of the EEC's "stock in trade" in all the various institutional forms that the Union took in the following years.

Trade and production *play a decisive role in the international competitiveness of the EU Member States. Their "financing" requires massive investment to improve the quality of human life. Given the tight budgetary constraints imposed on governments, there is an increasing need for private sector investment in large-scale projects.*

One area with significant "economic" implications, where the impact of EU rules can be assessed in advance, is certainly that of "public" procurement.

Infrastructure *constitutes a large part of a country's public capital and the essence of* ***investing for the long-term in Europe****.*

Moreover, the fiscal policy of a country is certainly a significant factor in choosing the location of an investment, but it is not the only one, nor necessarily the most important. The geographical accessibility of markets, infrastructure, the cost and functionality of transport, environmental standards, availability and quality of the workforce, wage levels, social security systems and government policies are equally crucial elements in ***investment decisions****.*

Historically, activity related to the ***construction of infrastructure*** *has been a major concern for public authorities, given its importance in terms of use and cost.*

For this reason, the systems for building infrastructure and all public works are inevitably an area where EU regulatory principles are absolutely dominant in forging a common rule-book, a "corpus" that makes public procurement rules uniform across the Member States and for the UK a significant part of the EU ***derived domestic legislation*** *[as such confirming its "effect in domestic law on and after the exit day",* ***EUWA****, sec. 2 (1B)].*

Public Procurement

The various **regulatory principles** on competitiveness in procurement (of works, services or supplies) are an expression of the more general principles of the Treaties. Although the Treaties do not contain specific provisions in this respect, they lay down four fundamental principles which can also be applied to public procurement:

- prohibition of discrimination on grounds of nationality (Art. 18 TFEU);
- free movement of goods (Art. 34 TFEU);
- free access to services (Art. 56 TFEU).

The application of these principles requires that *"competitive neutrality"* be ensured in public sector activities by creating a *"level playing field for firms across the EU to bid for tenders that, in aggregate, approximate 14% of EU GDP per annum"* [P.B. Whyman, A.I. Petrescu (2017)].

> *"Public procurement law is a highly technical field of law, long guided by a seemingly straightforward ideal: ensuring that the government uses public funds most cost-effectively in providing public services. In the European Union (EU) context, it is a niche area of internal market law where the objectives are slightly more expansive and refer to the integration of markets and their 'opening-up to undistorted competition in all the Member States'"* [S. BOGOJEVIĆ, in S. BOGOJEVIĆ, X. GROUSSOT, J. HETTNE (2019)].

For the above mentioned reasons, the EU Directives on public works adopted over the years contain a number of provisions governing procedures for selecting contractors for procurement. They provide a precise list of the actors obliged to apply these laws.

The scope of EU regulations is limited to the phase prior to the execution of public works, leaving the execution phase to the discretion of Member States' national legislation.

The way in which the **regulations** provide for the selection of contractors is inspired by the achievement of maximum competitiveness, in the sense that the EU requires calls for tenders to select the contractors who will carry out the public works.

The *Preamble* to Dir 2014/24/EU on public procurement sets out the principles underpinning the legislation.

> *"The award of public contracts by or on behalf of Member States' authorities has to comply with the principles of the Treaty on the Functioning of the European Union (TFEU), and in particular the free movement of goods, freedom of establishment and the freedom to provide services, as well as the principles deriving therefrom, such as equal treatment, non-discrimination, mutual recognition, proportionality and transparency."*

The procedures used by government offices to select contractors are termed *open, restricted* and *negotiated* procedures.

In the selection procedures for contractors, since the objective is to promote **competitiveness**, the general rule is that contracting entities are encouraged to use "open" more than "restricted" bidding, while "negotiated" procedures (with or without publication of the call for tender) refer to cases in which contracting authorities' offices may contact the companies of their choice and negotiate future contracts directly. This is allowed in exceptional or urgent cases, or when irregular, unacceptable or inappropriate offers have been submitted in a previous open or restricted procedure.

Procurement (and public procedures for procurement) is actually an area in which one of the central issues of the modern state is at stake: how *"confining, structuring and checking discretion"* [K.C. DAVIS (1971)] can be accomplished without hindering the efficient performance of public activities (or in professor Davis' words *"how to avoid the growth of unnecessary discretionary power, and how to control necessary discretion power"* [K.C. DAVIS (1976)]).

This leaves ample room for policies that promote highly individualized and *'partnership-based'* contracting models involving long-term co-operative relationships. Furthermore, it reflects a long-standing legacy of contracting,

> *"in which the emphasis has increasingly been on the role of relationality in contracts, characterized by norms promoting values including flexibility, reciprocity, and solidarity"* [T. PROSSER (2014)].

The emphasis on relationality can also be seen as a legacy of *"common law fashioning a rule to enhance economic efficiency"* [P. CRAIG (2015)].

Policies and Procedures

EU regulations on public procurement are of considerable complexity and enormous importance in providing a more structured and open system for the *award* of *public contracts*.

With regard to *policies*, contracting is not simply a matter of getting the best value for money. Policies also raise issues of **equal treatment** and other social **environment concerns** (values which are considered essential to achieve *sustainable development*).

A system's overall productivity depends to a large extent on the external economy supported by **public infrastructure**, based on the fundamental objective of a synergetic approach to economic, social and environmental policy.

In this context, environmental protection must be taken as a fundamental component of a dynamic economy. Governments can draw up technical specifications for the characteristics of the works, supplies and contracted services that take into account environmental values.

The contribution of EU public procurement law to the implementation of the **internal market** is conspicuous:

> *"EU law governing public procurement is significantly more detailed and sophisticated in the control it exercises over national autonomy than is general internal market law. On all three counts – the substance of the control imposed on national regulatory discretion, the procedural dimensions of national administrative practice and remedies – EU public procurement law is a great deal more intricate. It confines and channels national practice in a much more precise way than does primary law, thereby to challenge more robustly abuse of discretionary powers to award contracts that are held by public authorities at national and regional level"*[S. WEATHERILL, in S. BOGOJEVIĆ *et al.* (2019)].

Compared to other areas of the internal market, EU public procurement law has its own critical features:

> *"It depends heavily on its Member States to implement the rules and, ideally, to entrench them in local administrative practice. It seems, however, that obstacles to the functioning of the internal market caused by local culture, preferences and tradition persist. So the directives on public procurement put in place much more concrete and detailed rules, under an assumption that the true potential of the internal market cannot be realised without deeper cuts into national autonomy than are envisaged by the rules of primary EU law alone, and yet their impact seems to be weak. Top-down law-making is not transformative"* [*Ibid*].

These **procedures** are also too restrictive as they focus on individual contracts to the detriment of longer-term relations with contractors, but their existence is one of the reasons why transparency is far greater than in the past.

The EU's "traditional" approach to public procurement has been modernized with the introduction of *"Dynamic Purchasing Systems"* or *"completely electronic buying systems for current purchases"*.

In terms of *organizational instruments*, two main features must be highlighted:

- the establishment at national level of *central procurement offices*, as a government procurement office that purchases supplies and/or services for other procurement offices, or that takes on

the characteristics of a dual organizational model, i.e. purchasing and brokerage structures;
- the establishment of an *electronic market*, conceived of as a real virtual market *(e-procurement)* accessible at a dedicated website where government offices – choosing from similar products – can purchase what best meets their needs.

In terms of new *contractual instruments*, the main features are:

- *framework agreements*, stipulated by one or more government procurement offices and one or more economic operators with a view to concluding contracts to be awarded during a given period, where necessary, at fixed prices and quantities;
- *competitive dialogue*, in which any economic operator may participate: the procuring office initiates a dialogue with the candidates admitted to the procedure with the aim of finding one or more solutions to meeting requirements, which are then used as criteria for inviting the selected candidates to submit bids. The procedure in this case is characterized by greater flexibility with the aim of allowing contracting agencies to "dialogue" with the participating companies in order to design a bid closer to the needs of the contracting agency.

Contracting Authorities

Entities governed by public law are included in the category of so-called "contracting authorities", i.e. those actors who are obliged to apply *legal procedures* in *the award of contracts* for public works.

In order to focus on the issue, it is necessary to consider the "public" nature of these entities within the EU legal order.

A **substantive** concept of **public entity** has been developed in EU law: on this basis private or public ownership is irrelevant for determining whether it should be defined as a body governed by public law.

The current approach was achieved through EU legislation after a long process that began with the first directives in this area (1971). The directives' scope of application was limited to "formally" public entities, i.e. institutional actors charged with protecting the interests of the community: state and local governments and public legal entities (state universities, scientific and cultural institutions, welfare agencies, etc.).

However, it was immediately noted that the EU concept of a public actor based entirely on purely "formal" criteria gave rise to an opportunity to easily circumvent the obligations laid down in EU directives on contracts by entities which, albeit formally private, carried out activities with public implications.

This led to the decision to extend the concept of "public" legal person in EU legislation. Several criteria – not purely formal– were introduced to identify which actors are obliged to adhere to procurement laws. *Body governed by public law* is therefore the reformulated concept of the "substantive" notion of the contracting authority.

An actor can be considered a "body governed by public law" if three basic requisites are met.

The first is to be endowed with legal personality.

The other two are more complex in their definition.

- One is carrying out activities designed to meet needs of *general interest*, i.e. the activity must meet general needs that are not of an industrial or commercial nature. In this regard, it is not necessary that all the entity's activity is aimed at the fulfilment of non-business ends.

> *"Thus laws concerning public procurement may operate in conjunction with competitive conduct laws in regulating the potentially anti-competitive impact of commercial purchasing activities by public authorities"* [K. YEUNG, in M. FREEDLAND *et al.* (2006)].

What characterizes the body in question is the fact that it is set up to pursue non-entrepreneurial public interests, which does not *per se* exclude the possibility that it carries out other activities, including those of an industrial or commercial nature:

- The other is that the activity financed by state, local authorities, public bodies or other public entities (*the majority of public financing*), or management is subject to control by such entities (*majority public control*).

The two requirements set out above are to be considered as alternatives. In other words, the existence of only *one of the two latter requisites* (non-business public activity or public financing) is sufficient to qualify an actor as a *body governed by public law*.

Effects of the Withdrawal

Current UK public procurement legislation *derives* entirely from the *transposition* of the latest generation of EU directives.

The *Public Contracts Regulations* 2015 (as amended), the *Utilities Contract Regulations* 2016 and the *Concession Contracts Regulations* 2016 incorporated Directives n. 2014/24/ EU, 2014/23/ EU and 2015/25/ EU respectively into national law for England and Wales, taking a *copy out* approach, that is to say that, as far as possible, the **text** of the regulation is the **same** as the directive it implements (similarly Scotland, which has its own jurisdiction, adopted the *Public Contracts (Scotland) Regulations 2006*).

The EU Directives and the UK Regulations also establish special enforcement procedures providing judicial remedies for disappointed suppliers and contractors. The courts have assumed an increasingly important role in "*procurement matters as a result of the remedies sought there under the EU public contracts rules*" [T. PROSSER (2014)]. *Remedies* include suspension of a contract's award and its ineffectiveness or annulment for serious procedural breaches. The court may also award damages, and a suspension period (stand-still clause) between the decision awarding the contract and its signature, if necessary, to allow the provision of information on which to base an appeal.

In the context of the "*Separation Provisions*" of the **Withdrawal Agreement,** the provisions on public procurement (Article 75 to 77) regulated "ongoing" procedures, e.g. procedures launched by contracting authorities of the Member States or the UK on the basis of the general principles of EU law applicable to the award of public contracts.

The provisions ensured *continuity* in the application of EU law governing public procurement procedures in the Transition Period and compliance with the "*non-discrimination principle*" in ongoing procedures.

Now that the transition period has expired, the UK has the possibility to *redesign public procurement rules* according to perceived economic development needs.

As noted (*supra* Introduction), all EU derived legislation – such as procurement rules – remains under the ***European Union (Withdrawal) Act*** (EUWA) in force until repealed or amended by internal legislation.

With respect to the application of the transposed rules, the EU-WA, however, disapplies

> *"the supremacy of EU law, ending the preliminary reference procedure to the CJEU and ensuring that transposed EU procurement law will continue to have effect as domestic law"* [C. MADDOX (2019)].

As regards the interpretation of "retained" EU law – as already seen – it will have

> *"to be decided in accordance with relevant retained case law and retained EU law principles. [...] The Supreme Court may depart from retained EU case law by applying the same test it would apply when determining whether to depart from its own case law"* [*Ibid*].

Over time, EU procurement legislation will continue to evolve and the two (originally identical) procurement regimes may therefore have *different legislative developments* and *compatibility* between the *two regimes* may cease.

The Procurement Regime in the *Trade and Cooperation Agreement*

A new regulatory framework is likely to result from the UK's accession to the WTO *Government Procurement Agreement* (GPA). The choice was foreseen in the **Political Declaration**:

> *"Noting the United Kingdom's intention to accede to the WTO Government Procurement Agreement (GPA), the Parties should provide for mutual opportunities in the Parties' respective public procurement markets beyond their commitments under the GPA in areas of mutual interest, without prejudice to their domestic rules to protect their essential security interests"* (sec. 46).

The GPA regulates the basis on which WTO Members give access to their markets, aiming essentially at the mutual opening of public procurement markets on the basis of common principles of *transparency, competition*, *equal treatment* and *reasoned decision* in the award of contracts:

> *"Although the GPA contains less detail, it appears to be based on very similar principles to the current EU procurement regime. If the UK were to adopt the GPA approach, it would be possible for contracting authorities and suppliers to adjust to this regime, although it would not be a seamless transition. One downside is that in terms of procurement market access, access to EU procurement markets would be more restricted than it is currently, as the scope of GPA coverage of EU procurement markets is narrower than it is for EU member states.* […] *Looking ahead, it is also possible that the GPA may well, over time, evolve in a similar direction to the EU procurement regime"* [C. MADDOX (2019)].

Beyond the mutual aspiration to cooperate, this is an area in which limits are set by territorial *borders*: while EU rules will be inevitable for UK economic operators bidding on EU territory, the future alignment remains limited to a non-binding commitment – stated in the Political Declaration – to

> *"standards based on those of the GPA ensuring transparency of market opportunities* (…)*. Building on these standards, the Parties should address the risk of arbitrary behaviour when awarding contracts, and make available remedies and review procedures, including before judicial authorities"* (sec. 47).

At the same time, reconciling the different regulatory frameworks is relevant for the **global legal order**.

In this context, GPA rules

> *"conceived as a means for promoting the free circulation of goods and services,* […] *on the basis of open tendering procedures applied in a non-discriminatory manner"* [may be even] *"conceived so as to harmonize domestic goal of protection with global demands for free trade"* [S. CASSESE (2018)].

On its side, the EU's objective was to strengthen the envisaged partnership by providing:

> *"for mutual opportunities in the Parties' respective public procurement markets* […] *beyond their commitments under the GPA in specific areas* […]*. These areas should include relevant procurement not covered by the GPA such as procurement in the utilities sectors not covered under the GPA. National treatment should ensure treatment no less favourable than that accorded to locally-established suppliers or service providers"* [**Directives for negotiation**, sec. 54].

The expectation– in the interest of both parties – to maintain mutual standards in the awarding of contracts appears to be confirmed by the regulations which apply to the area in the **Trade and Cooperation Agreement**. While according to the premise, the UK can develop a separate and **independent public procurement regime**, the TCA provides for a **framework** of transparent and non-discriminatory **rules** in public procurement (Part 2, Title VI).

The rules are based on the GPA, but include some additions to address the non-covered issues noted above, including the use of *electronic means, electronic publication of notices, environmental, social and labour considerations* and *domestic review procedures*.

Future UK domestic developments, tabled in the expanded GPA framework, could contribute to an evolution of **global rules** in the area, harmonising – as mentioned above – the *"domestic goal of protection with global demands for free trade"*.

Private Contract Litigation

The *private contracts* sector raises questions that are no less intriguing than in the public contracts field. Over 75% of EU-27 *capital market business* is conducted through the UK and as a result the UK provides an important (the most important) **private legal infrastructure** for business in Europe and the **leading** international dispute **resolution centre**. The choice of **English law** and **jurisdiction** has so far prevailed over any other applicable law in recent decades.

Particular attention will be required – in this context – for financial market transactions between UK companies and their counterparties in the EU: under several EU laws there is an obligation to submit any dispute to a court in an EU Member State.

London is currently also the most important centre of legal activities for *companies in distress* that need to restructure their financial assets. As the transition period has now expired, court decisions on *insolvency proceedings* will not be automatically recognised throughout the EU.

A signal was already given by the communication of the *European Stability Mechanism* (ESM), which since October 2019 has switched to Luxembourg law for bonds issued to financially support Eurozone member countries in difficulty. These bonds were, in fact, previously governed by English law:

> *"The ESM's move is part of a broader shift among European issuers towards contracts governed by continental law. EU banks have begun selling more domestic-law bonds, worrying that after Brexit, debt governed by English law may no longer satisfy the requirements of regulators"* [T. STUBBINGTON, in *Financial Times,* 26 September 2019].

Jurisdiction and Enforcement

In the EU legal order, *choice of law* and *the choice of forum* clauses are governed by the *Directive* 593/2008 on contractual obligations, named *Rome I*; *Directive* 564/2007 on non-contractual obligations, *Rome II*; and *Directive* 1215/2012 on jurisdiction, recognition and enforcement of judgments in civil and commercial matters, *Brussels Ia*. The overall effect is that choice of *law*, *jurisdiction* and *enforcement* are the same across the EU. Now that *Rome I, II* and *Brussels Ia* have ceased to have effect for UK courts,

> *"as a consequence, choice of law and jurisdiction will no longer be subject to the same regime* [...] *The worst thing, however, is that parties cannot trust anymore that choice of law and choice of forum clauses will be equally enforced in the UK and the remaining Member States"* [G. RÜHL, in J. ARMOUR, H. EIDENMÜLLER (2017)].

The issue is also relevant for enforcement in EU cross-border *insolvency proceedings*, which are currently regulated by Regulation 2015/848 of 20 May 2015. According to this regulation, judgments given in judicial proceedings by the competent courts are recognized in other Member States. In this respect, EU rules

> *"endorse the principle of automatic recognition, which matches that of mutual trust governing the relationships between the courts of Member States"* [A. LEANDRO, R. VAN GALEN, in L. GHIA (2019)].

Maintaining the *status quo* on all the above mentioned issues will not be automatic. Given that the various procedural legal frameworks are not addressed in the **TCA,** a future agreement will not be simple and, in any case, will take a long time. An alternative would be for the UK to replace the EU regime with a more **global legal framework**.

The prospects here are complex, as there is currently *no compre-*

hensive legal framework for *litigation*. In the **UK's Approach to negotiations**, reference is made to *"multilateral precedents set by the Hague Conference on Private International Law"*, despite the fact that the Hague Conference does not cover choice of law, but only choice of jurisdiction.

In the current context, an urgent issue concerns the **enforcement** of judgments. The rulings of the EU-27 Courts could so far be effectively enforced in the UK, as permitted by *Brussels Ia* (Article 42(i)), in favour of the beneficiary of a judgment delivered in one Member State and which has to be enforced in another Member State. As of January 1, 2021, rulings issued by UK courts are considered judgments of third country courts throughout the EU (and reciprocally). There is no provision in the **TCA** that clarifies whether civil court judgments will be recognized. The issue therefore remains unresolved.

The **TCA** does not address the issue except for some very limited provisions on *legal services* (Part 2, Title II, Chapter 5, Section VII), which allow a "third country" lawyer to act under their own "*home jurisdiction professional title*" (with no guarantee of mutual recognition of qualifications) and the (broader) provisions on "*Law enforcement* and *Judicial cooperation in criminal matters*", *Part* 3).

Unlike the previous areas of regulation considered above, for which more than four decades of membership enabled legal culture and practice to largely contribute to the **foundations** of the **joint regulatory framework,** the area of litigation and private law enforcement remains entrusted to the capacity of the Parties to handle all relevant issues in terms of mutual *accountability*.

A more immediate prospect for the UK is access to the Lugano Convention, originally signed in 1988 between the EU and certain EFTA Member States (Iceland, Norway, Switzerland), to regulate cross-border jurisdiction and ensure recognition of court judgments. Access will however require a unanimous decision on the application submitted by the UK.

Chapter 6
EQUIVALENCE

"Our Britain seems as of it, but not in't;
In a great pool a swan's nest: printhee, think
There's livers out of Britain"
(SHAKESPEARE, Cymbeline,
Act III, Scene IV, 140)

Building Leadership in Financial Market Regulation

Imogene, Cymbeline's proud daughter, refers her words to a wider picture: the "world's volume" of which Britain seems "as of it, but not in it". To arrive at a more limited contemporary framework, playing "in" and "not in it" says a lot about Britain's history in Europe from the time of its accession and throughout the last forty-six years.

In this chapter, referring to capital and banking markets, the issue is precisely not about being "in" or "out", but rather about having been "in" and, at the same time, "not in it".

As is well known, Cymbeline is the mythical king of Britain in imperial Roman times (derived from the medieval legends – written in Latin – by Geoffrey of Monmouth, "Historia Regnum Britanniae"), who ended his victorious war against Rome with the peaceful recognition of the Roman Empire:

> *"To all our subjects. Set we forward: let / A Roman and a British ensign wave / Friendly together"* [Act V, Scene V, 480].

The idea of "ensigns" waving to each other has been framed in a multiplicity of institutional arrangements to maintain a kind of ***common regulatory framework for financial services****, albeit with all the long-standing differences in supervisory matters.*

British dominance *over the* ***European financial world*** *has been a long process. The establishment of a financed national debt centred on* *the Bank of England dates back to 1694, a few years after the Glorious Revolution, with all its "emphasis on exceptionalism (the notion that the country was distinctive)" [J. BLACK (2019)].*

The "Great Bank of Europe" was then the result of the post-Napoleonic European political order, which lasted until the recent European Banking Union (which began in October 2014, exactly two centuries later). The new EU institutional framework marks the definitive emergence of a supranational authority that deals not only with the single currency but also with banking supervision.

This event probably implies the dissolution of that "looser Union sort" that Edmond Burke called the ***Commonwealth of Europe*** *and which, in the end, allowed the United Kingdom to* ***remain "in"*** *the EU financial markets and* ***"not in it"****.*

With the emergence of the European Central Bank as a single authority for currency and financial supervision, the Churchillian vision of Britain's destiny to help shape Europe reversed. This posed the risk that the former would be shaped by Europe.

However, once again ***EU financial regulation*** *owes much to the UK: the UK's stature as a financial services centregave it considerable influence over the creation of EU regulations throughout its membership period.*

In the era that began on January 1, 2021, transition period legal concepts such as ***mutual recognition*** *and* ***equivalence*** *will play a central role (with all their multiple interpretations) in "rebuilding" a new relationship, but even more in defining the area of* ***competing policies*** *for* ***leadership*** *in the* ***regulation*** *of the financial services sector.*

Building a Unified Financial Market

Going back to history,

> *"Modern public finance emerged in northern Italy around the Renaissance. For the first time, states were run by merchants, not soldiers".* [Their finances relied on the idea that]*"interest would be paid if the government's finance were healthy enough* [...] *The model was improved in rigor and reliability by other city-states in northern Europe"* [D. DODD (2014)].

Similar practices immediately spread throughout Europe. **Public debt securities** (i.e. negotiable transferable financial instruments issued to the general public) became the real money of credit. *"Wars – the most relevant precedent – were financed by increases in public debt"* [M. DRAGHI, *We face a war against coronavirus and must mobilise accordingly*, in *Financial Times*, 25 March 2020].

The close relationship between **sovereign debt** and **banking** belongs instead to our times.

Over the last century continental banks have been quite willing to develop close and lasting ties with industry, securing influence by participating in the boards of these companies, while British banks – since the Victorian era – excelled in short-term commercial banking (e.g. discounting bills, deposits and clearing) and in general in "merchant banking" (such as shipping and trade finance). The banking functions that evolved in France, Germany and Italy usually included a wider variety of activities and were defined as "universal banks", based on long-term relationships with companies.

Continental banks heavily involved in large companies and lending to particular industrial sectors were more exposed to banking crises during industrial crises.

Consequently, although the Treaty of Rome explicitly provides for the *free movement of capital*, the need to protect their financial institutions from foreign competition or the fear that unlimited movement of capital mobility would be responsible for repeated banking crises prevented the mobility of capital. At the beginning of the 1960s partial liberalisation began, including several safeguard clauses. It was only with the *Maastricht Treaty* that all national restrictions on the movement of capital were removed, except those on grounds of national security.

However, efforts to build a **unified financial market** (including all the activities undertaken in the financial system, e.g. by banks, asset managers, and insurance companies) in Europe go back a long time. The main steps have been: the abolition of restrictions on freedom to **establish banks** and other financial institutions (1973); the introduction of the **home country control principle** (1977) (the home country of the parent bank is responsible for supervising the bank's activities in other EU countries); the principle that any entity authorized in one EU country may open branches or provide **cross-border financial services** in other EU countries (1989); the adoption of the *Financial Ser-*

vices Action Plan (FSAP) in 1999, a plan calling for the harmonisation of prudential rules and the creation of a **single market** for wholesale financial services and efforts to unify the retail market.

The global financial crisis revealed the weakness of existing macro-prudential oversight in the EU and

> *"the inadequacy of nationally-based supervisory models in overseeing integrated financial markets with cross-border operators"* [D. HOWARTH, L. QUAGLIA, in C.J. BICKERTON *et al.* (2015)].

It also revealed fundamental weaknesses in the central banks' own assessment of management capacity and risk (*risk sensitivity*).

A crisis of confidence hit central banks, including the *Bank of England*, in the face of the crises experienced by banks (Northern Rock or the Royal Bank of Scotland) that called for public bailouts. The financial crisis accentuated the need to have *risk-management institutions* at all levels and, more generally, structural restrictions on intermediaries to limit the ability of financial entities to be too large or too interconnected to fail with a consequent moral hazard profile. In the light of these events, the EU began to *redefine the rules*, also involving the UK financial market.

As is rightly noted:

> *"Although the UK financial market is in many respects distinct from other EU27 markets, being significantly larger and hosting the deepest wholesale market, many of its governing rules are set by the EU and the EU is also increasingly shaping how supervision is carried out"* [N. MOLONEY, in M. DOUGAN (2017)].

EU Supervisory Institutions

At the institutional level, the process of establishing a **network** of macro- and micro-prudential supervisors started with the establishment of the *European Systemic Risk Board* (ESRB), which became operative in December 2010. The board is chaired by the president of the ECB and its mandate is the macro-prudential oversight of the EU financial system and the prevention and mitigation of systemic risk. In pursuing this mandate, the ESRB monitors and assesses systemic risks and, where appropriate, issues warnings and recommendations (the mandate was recently updated by Regulation (EU) 2019/2176 of 18 December 2019). Besides the recommending role of the ESRB, an appropriate macro- and micro-prudential regulatory system in the form of the *European System of Financial Supervision* (ESFS) entered into force in 2011.

A group of three independent EU institutions at sectoral level is responsible for micro-prudential supervision and coordination of the different national supervisory authorities carrying out day-to-day supervision: the *European Banking Authority* (EBA), with its headquarters established in London (and moved to Paris after the 2016 referendum), the *European Securities and Markets Authority* (ESMA), already located in Paris, and the *European Insurance and Occupational Pensions Authority* (EIOPA), based in Frankfurt. The *Joint Committee of European Supervisory Authorities* (ESAs) is responsible for cross-sectorial coordination and consistency between the three institutions and the different *National Competent Authorities* (NCAs). The three institutions also develop draft regulatory technical standards and implement technical standards in their respective areas.

The EBA, in particular, monitors supervision by national authorities, acts as a mediator in disagreements between competent authorities and provides advice to the European institutions.

On the other hand the first steps towards a *banking union* were taken in 2012 with the agreement to create a ***Single Supervisory Mechanism*** **(SSM)** and a ***Single Resolution Mechanism*** **(SRM)**. The objective of the *banking union* is to break the relationship between **sovereign** and **bank debt** by providing unified supervision and rules for Eurozone banks. The process of harmonising *supervisory*, *resolution*, and *deposit insurance* regulatory frameworks began in spring 2013 with the new *Supervisory Rule Book* based on Basel III, the *Bank Recovery and Resolution Directive* Directive 2014/59, and the *Deposit Guarantee Schemes Directive* Directive 2014/49.

At the end of the above summarized process:

> *"The EU has grown more visible and influential in global financial regulation. Three factors underpinned this trend: the emergence and growing coherence of a truly European capital market aided by the single currency; the further concentration of regulatory capacity in supranational hands; and the partial delegitimization of US governance and rules through the stock market crash and high-profile scandals of the early 2000s"* [D. MÜGGE (2014)].

Since its inception, the SSM has been responsible for the prudential **supervision of credit institutions** in the Eurozone in cooperation with the NCAs in order to ensure the safety and soundness of credit institutions and financial stability. It became the key institution in the micro- and macro-prudential supervision of Eurozone banking institutions in close cooperation with national supervisors and other ESFS institutions, in particular the EBA.

In contrast, the SRM has **resolution powers** to minimize the cost of bank failures to the taxpayer and to the economy at large and operates within the same regulatory framework as the SSM. It consists of a *Single Resolution Board* (SRB) and a *Single Resolution Fund* (SRF).

The banking union project is incomplete due to the lack of a pan-European **insolvency regime** and the lack of a **common deposit insurance system**, which are controversial as they imply a greater degree of fiscal union among Eurozone countries.

UK Supervisory Institutions

The UK's approach has been characterised over time by constant resistance to unified European financial regulation, from both the financial services industry and the government. The latter's list of complaints includes several legal challenges to EU financial regulation before the Court of Justice of the European Union (CJEU) – for instance – on issues such as *prohibitions or conditions on short selling* (the UK contested the ESMA's authority to temporarily suspend short-selling of financial instruments, but lost the case, C-270/12 *UK v European Parliament and Council*).

None of the agreements or treaties relating to **supervisory institutions** were signed by the UK. Nor did the UK participate in the creation of the ESM (*infra* Ch. 7) which was set up outside the EU framework because non-euro countries were not interested in financing this mechanism – aimed at safeguarding the stability of the euro area – either directly or indirectly (e.g. the UK participated in the Irish bailout through bilateral loans).

In this regard, while the opt-out from the *European Monetary Union* (*infra* Ch. 7) and from *Fiscal Policy* (*infra* Ch. 8) hindered the UK's influence on monetary and economic policy and Schengen had an impact on social and cohesion policy, the refusal to join the *single supervisory institutions* had a strong effect – even before the UK left the EU – on capital and banking markets:

> *"As the UK is not participating in the SRM, its banking system will not contribute to funding the SRF. Instead, the Bank of England will have access to a resolution fund out of the existing bank levies on liabilities. The fact that the UK remains outside the SRM may hamper its effectiveness given that large European banks have important parts of their operation in London and the relevance of London as an international financial center"* [X. VIVES (2016)].

In short, although the UK participated in some areas of financial integration, it remained outside of every important area of regulation, specifically *supervisory* and *resolution procedures.*

As the UK is the most important financial centre for euro-denominated transactions, strengthening the governance of Eurozone financial markets potentially threatened the UK's role in European finance. The European Central Bank (ECB) attempted to shift the settlement of euro-denominated transactions to the euro area. The UK brought the case before the CJEU on the assumption that this violated the single market provision on the free movement of capital. The Court supported the UK [CJEU, Case T – 496/11 *United Kingdom of Great Britain* and *Northern Ireland* v. *European Central Bank*, ECLI: EU: T: 2015:133]:

> *"The UK defended the interests of euro-outs as financial integration continued apace. The British government pressed for a double-majority voting system [of euro ins and euro-outs] in the EBA, as its extant majority system would have effectively allowed the euro area to govern the technical standards that would have been applied to all EU banks"* [M. CHANG, in F. FABBRINI (2017)].

After the 2016 UK referendum the EU Commission decided to move **clearing activities** to the EU as part of its plans to reform the *European Market Infrastructure Regulation* (EMIR). There is a degree of supranational sovereignty in having the euro-market located within the Eurozone, especially considering the existence of a large market for financial products denominated in the single currency.

With the attribution of banking supervisory powers to the SSM (formally an ECB unit, but essentially autonomous), the process resulted in the establishment of a transnational supervisory system due to the transfer of shares of national sovereignty: the ESFS gives rise to a '"system architecture" representing the evolution of **unified rules** and supervisory authorities for the Eurozone as a whole.

The result is the development of a **European supervisory system** which is currently the **largest financial supervisor in the western world.** The system strengthens cooperation and coordination mechanisms through supranational powers. National responsibility for banking supervision by the NCAs is residual with regard to *less significant banks*.

The UK "Light touch" Regulatory Approach

The UK has its own regulatory system. Until 2012, the supervisory system was based on the *Financial Services Authority* (FSA) model, in which an independent integrated regulator authorized and supervised financial institutions and securities and was responsible for the solvency problems of individual institutions. The financial crisis led to *"a crisis of confidence"* [D. CONAGHAN (2012)] after the *"innocence lost"* (according to the former Governor of the Bank of England [M. KING (2016)].

The FSA was abolished with the reforms of financial regulatory institutions implemented by the *Financial Services Act 2012*, and FSAs' responsibilities were divided between two new agencies: the *Prudential Regulation Authority* (PRA, a subsidiary of the Bank of England) responsible for prudential regulation and supervision of financial entities, and the independent *Financial Conduct Authority* (FCA), dedicated to consumer protection and promoting competition in the financial sector but with a subordinated role to the competition authority (CMA). The PRA has a key role in *bailout* agreements, *recovery* and *resolution* regimes, and *regulatory capital.* It can introduce rules requiring a bank to prepare a "recovery plan" or a "resolution plan," and can impose strict controls after consultations with the Treasury, the Bank of England, and the FCA.

The famous **light-touch style** of regulation is respected by the FCA, ensuring that markets are regulated, taking into account the operational objectives of consumer protection, integrity, and competition:

> *"There are some welcome increases in transparency in the new model, which may also do something to clarify the different responsibilities of*

> *each of the institutional actors involved"* [and not to reconfigure] *"a risk-based model* […] *to avoid the over-confidence of the past"* [T. PROSSER (2014)].

The new banking regulation measures include the *Special Liquidity Scheme* to improve liquidity and increase market confidence, the *Credit Guarantee Scheme* to secure bank debt on wholesale markets, and the *Asset Protection Scheme* to protect against future credit losses on certain assets.

The cultural foundation of the UK's current regulatory approach can be seen as the result of a balance between a *prudential approach* and a *judgment-led approach to regulation*, so as to maintain an advantage in competing with other global financial hubs i.e. true competitors with London's financial centre (New York, Hong-Kong, and Singapore).

Interconnections in Financial Markets

As is well known, the financial sector is the *most interconnected in the world*.

"Disentangling" is a term that has already been used for utility regulatory regimes (*supra* Ch. 4) and which may also be used in this context. Official positions since the pre-referendum period appear to have been aware of the point.

It has long been clear that:

> *"the UK government would need to disentangle the regulatory framework from EU law for the financial sector. Regardless of the exit negotiations outcome this would be a large and complex task"* [H.M. UK Government (2016)].

The issue arises from the fact that although the UK did not participate in the EU's institutional supervisory framework:

> *"For most types of financial services, EU law amounts to the substantial majority of the UK's legislative framework, whether directly applicable or EU Directives transposed into UK law. EU Directives and Regulations govern the regulation – both prudential and conduct of business of all major sectors, including banking, insurance, wholesale and retail investments, provision of market infra-*

> *structure, payment, clearing and settlement systems and a host of other activities"* [*Ibid*].

Thus, with the UK **in "it"**, but **"not in it"** the EU financial regulatory system gave rise (before exit day) to *intertwined* and *mixed* (somewhat confusing) **regulatory oversight** of Europe's most important financial centre.

Consequently, the point was:

> *"how to avoid regulatory gaps in the UK's domestic legislative framework once the EU Treaties ceased to apply. This would involve questions over how existing EU law could or should be adopted into domestic law"* [*Ibid*].

Thanks to "passporting", during the transition period UK financial companies – including banks, insurers and asset managers have had the right to sell financial services anywhere in the EU without other countries imposing different or additional requirements. The loss of "passports" now deprives financial institutions of the cross-border market access they have enjoyed in vital sectors such as corporate credit and insurance. Mutually, EU-based financial companies will require regulatory approval to operate in the UK.

According to another UK official document:

> *"In our new strategic partnership agreement we will be aiming for the freest possible trade in financial services between the UK and EU Member States.*
> *In highly integrated sectors such as financial services there will be a legitimate interest in mutual cooperation arrangements that recognize the interconnectedness of markets, as so clearly demonstrated by the financial crisis. Since that time, the EU has taken a number of steps to strengthen collective oversight of the sector"* [H.M. UK Government (2017)].

Given the clear mutual interest in maintaining **connectivity** between the two financial markets, the central importance of interconnection between the UK and EU financial markets was officially reaffirmed during the withdrawal process:

> *"UK-located banks underwrite around half of the debt and equity issued by EU businesses; UK-located banks are counterparty to over half*

of the over-the-counter interest rate derivatives traded by EU companies and banks; around £1.4 trillion of assets are managed in the UK on behalf of European clients; the world-leading London Market for insurance hosts all of the world's twenty largest international (re)insurance companies; and more international banking activity is booked in the UK than in any other country" [**White Paper** *(July 2018)*].

The above figures form the basis for depicting the UK's financial role as a **global public good**:

"the UK is host to all 30 global systemically important banks and is the home regulator for four of them. Given its scale, the International Monetary Fund (IMF) has described financial stability in the UK as a "global public good". Alongside its European partners, the UK has developed an institutional framework to manage financial stability while ensuring the regulatory system supports a global financial centre" [*Ibid*].

On the other hand, there is a European community forged by the **common currency** that could increasingly find its interests in financial policy not aligned with the UK's interests, given the UK's intent to diverge in terms of financial regulation.

The Eurozone's banking union, which brought **banking supervision** and **resolution power** to the **supranational level**, strengthened this process. The UK government was – at the time – very risk-conscious, which is why it insisted that EBA decisions must be approved by a 'double majority' of both euro and non-euro countries in order to ensure 'safeguards' for the City of London.

The fear was that non-euro membership would leave the British financial industry at the mercy of rules laid down predominantly by the Eurogroup and that the UK government would be less and less able to exert influence over it.

The logical conclusion of this process has been the UK's concern that the financial services industry should live by **rules predominantly established by others**, according to a vision based on the assumption that it is the EMU legal system which sets the rules of the financial sector as a *de facto* collective entity and develops those rules differently from the point of view of a financial centre outside the common currency.

An Off-shore Perspective

For reasons of scale, liquidity and risk diversification, **capital markets** are inherently **global.** The City has had the advantage in the last decades of being both an *onshore* (its European membership allowed it to expand its onshore domestic market) and an *offshore* financial market.

Even without influence, and consequently with less dominance within the Eurozone market, the UK financial services sector can still do a thriving business with the rest of the world. It could, in other words, become the largest offshore financial centre in the world. Britain would effectively turn into a "Singapore upon the Thames" or a "Greater Guernsey".

The UK's financial system has the capacity to move on. The departure (in 1992) from the original form of currency coordination (as was the *Exchange Rate Mechanism*, *infra* Ch. 7), after the failure of the Bank of England's effort to support the sterling with the sale of its reserves,

> *"brought crucial benefits, enabling Britain, in fiscal independence from the EU, to manage its own finances and to become a leading offshore financial centre"* [J. BLACK (2019)].

As long as the UK remained in the EU it was subject to European majority decisions on its financial activities with the rest of the world. On the other hand, it is unlikely that the rest of the EU – and especially the Eurozone – will tolerate a *giant offshore financial centre* on its immediate borders.

Nevertheless, on the basis of a "fair" agreement, the parties envisaging the *"new partnership"* could still return to the legal framework of mutual recognition of the Shakespearian Roman and British "*ensign wave*".

Potential Regulatory Divergences

With the expiration of the transition period, interactions between the EU and UK financial systems will require a **respective type of recognition.**

The commitment to a "future partnership" in this area has been expressed by the European Council in the terms that the EU will seek

> *"to preserve financial stability, market integrity, investor and consumer protection and fair competition, while respecting the Parties' regulatory and decision-making autonomy, and their ability to take equivalence decisions in their own interest"* [Directives for Negotiation, sec. 44].

The above words are an expression of the EU institution's intention to steer the new partnership towards a **mutually acceptable regulatory framework** that allows for some sort of *regulatory divergence* without compromising *financial stability*.

A similar sentence can be found in the **Political Declaration**, which places at the heart of *"close and structured cooperation on regulatory and supervisory matters* […] *in their mutual interest"* […] *"the principles of regulatory autonomy"* (sec. 37).

Principles of **regulatory autonomy** will need to be reconciled with what is stated in the previous section, i.e.:

> *"that both Parties will have equivalence frameworks in place that allow them to declare a third country's regulatory and supervisory regimes equivalent for relevant purposes"* (sec. 36).

However, to avoid a mere verbal formula, this expectation must be filled in with specific provisions. The complexity of framing a relationship was even more clearly stated previously by the UK in the official position paper preparing for withdrawal:

> *"The EU has third country equivalence regimes which provide limited access for some of its third country partners to some areas of EU financial services markets. These regimes are not sufficient to deal with a third country whose financial markets are as deeply interconnected with the EU's as those of the UK are"* [**White Paper** *(July 2018)*].

In particular, – according to the quoted document – existing equivalence regimes do not provide for: a) *institutional dialogue*, meaning there is no bilateral mechanism for the EU and the third country to discuss *changes to their rules* on financial services; b) a *mediated solution* where equivalence is threatened by a *divergence of rules* or supervisory practices; c) sufficient tools for *reciprocal supervisory cooperation*; d) some *services*, where clients in the UK and the EU currently benefit from integrated markets and cross-border business models, with the effect of unnecessary *market fragmentation*; and e) gradual *adjustment* and careful management of the *impacts of change*, so that businesses face a predictable environment.

The Positions of the Parties

Whatever its limits, the application of the **equivalence regime** to third parties has a precondition: the authoritative *determination* that the third country's regulatory regime is equivalent to the EU regulatory architecture.

A comparison of rules is not necessarily the result of a balance between presumed "light" or "strong" regulation.

An example is the *Minimum Requirement for own funds and Eligible Liabilities* (MREL)), a typical and vital requirement for banks. In the Eurozone this requirement applies to banks with assets over €100bn, while in the US the threshold is $250bn, and in the UK the requirement starts at £15bn. The requirement is part of a set of rules introduced to isolate retail banks from investment bank risk and in this specific case the UK regulatory regime appears to use more prudential "loss-absorbency" criteria (as previously recommended by the *UK's Independent Commission on Banking*, Vickers Report, 2011).

In this scenario, the two legally relevant concepts for facilitating efficient and effective monitoring of cross-border activity are "**mutual recognition**" and "**equivalence**":

> *"'Mutual recognition' – a cornerstone principle of EU law* [...] *– is the approach to organizing cross-border financial market supervision most readily associated with the EU.* [...] *In broad strokes, mutual recognition allows an entity to operate cross-border on the basis of home country authorization and supervision"* [E. FERRAN, in D. MÜGGE (2014)].

The concepts of "equivalence" and "mutual recognition" are sometimes used interchangeably and have much in common:

> *"Equivalence shares with mutual recognition the notion that where there is an appropriate degree of similarity between different regulatory regimes, wasteful duplication can be avoided by giving concessions to actors potentially subject to multiple regimes. Equivalence implies a high degree of similarity".* [*Ibid*].

The question is whether *mutual recognition* can work in principle as a good way to address cross-border issues when (ultimately) regulatory frameworks may significantly diverge.

> *"The stumbling block is the degree of similarity that must exist be-*

> *tween systems for mutual recognition to operate safely and effectively. It has long been recognized that low-level similarity between systems is unlikely to be conducive to the development of the cross-border trust on which mutual recognition depends"* [*Ibid*].

The difference remains in operational terms, as mutual recognition has been fundamental to the creation of a single pan-EU internal market and operated basically among EU Member States.

For the UK, mutual recognition may be preferable given the scale and complexity of trade in financial services between the UK and the EU. The EU's official position stated by the European Council in issuing the **Directives for negotiation** for the new partnership was instead addressed uniquely to the **equivalence regime**:

> *"the key instrument the Parties will use to regulate interactions between their financial systems will be their respective unilateral equivalence frameworks"* [Directives for negotiation, sec. 44].

The wording used to characterize the regime should be noted: *"unilateral equivalence framework"*.

The point is further reaffirmed a few lines later, definitively clarifying the *"unilateral basis"* of the decision:

> *"Equivalence mechanisms and decisions remain defined and implemented on a unilateral basis by the European Union"* [Directives for negotiation, sec. 46].

The corresponding position of the UK, as recently stated, is much more general, and refers to the "future relationship" which will include

> *"legally binding obligations on market access and fair competition* [...] *by establishing regulatory cooperation arrangements that maintain trust and understanding between our autonomous systems of regulation as they evolve"* [UK's Approach to negotiations (2020), sec. 54-55].

In the **EU Draft Text**, reference is to "equivalence" without further clarification, merely mentioning that the Parties *"have committed to carrying out unilateral equivalence assessments for financial services"*. Confidence is expressed in the fact that they share the same rules and this *"provides a strong basis for concluding comprehensive equivalence assessments"* [Part 3, sec. 63].

The **UK Draft**, on the other hand, makes no mention of the need for an equivalence criterion. This perspective is evident in the definition of a general *"market access principle"*, according to which no party shall adopt measures imposing limitations on *"the number of cross-border financial service suppliers of the other party"*, on *"the total value of financial service transactions or assets"* and also on:

> *"the participation of foreign capital in terms of maximum percentage limit on foreign shareholding in financial service suppliers established in the territory of the Party"* [Chapter 17, Article 17.5].

A provision drafted without considering that *"participation of foreign capital"* has actually been broadly limited even in EU territory by the recent relaunch – after the pandemic shock – of "golden power" legislation in all Member States, in a context in which Member States have bailed out enterprises on an unprecedented scale.

Equivalence Decision-Making Process

The EU equivalence decision-making process is complex because it involves several EU institutions:

> *"Typically, the Commission, advised by ESMA, must adopt a positive equivalence decision before a Member State can choose to admit a third-country actor. Equivalence applies not only to formal regulatory equivalence, but also to third-country supervision and enforcement regimes"* [N. MOLONEY (2016)].

So far, equivalence has been actively applied within the frameworks governing third country actors' access to the EU in areas such as *accounting* and *auditing standards*, *rating agencies*, *hedge funds* and *market infrastructure*.

Indeed, given the *discretionary* nature of the judgment, the "unilateral" basis means that it is practically the ESMA which, in advising the Commission, is at the heart of a complex and politically sensitive determination on market access and will be able to exert its influence on the decision-making process. According to an authoritative opinion,

> *"ESMA is, by now, an experienced supervisor in certain capital market segments and may emerge from the Brexit negotiation period with en-*

> *hanced powers, whether in relation to the supervision of third country actors, equivalence determinations, or coordination with the global market"* [N. MOLONEY, in J. ARMOUR, H. EIDENMÜLLER (2017)].

Given the discretionary judgment involved, and its evolving structure (on the basis of actual divergence between the two regulatory regimes) it is consequent that, unlike goods or services, financial services have been left out of the negotiations on the future partnership. Market access will depend not on mutual agreement, but on a unilateral assessment by the EU (and reciprocally). On this basis, the possibility of regulatory equivalence in the trade deal under negotiation, has been firmly ruled out by the Commission

> *"As the Union's equivalence frameworks are unilateral, neither the equivalence assessments, nor possible decisions for granting equivalence are part of the negotiations with the United Kingdom. The current interconnectedness between the EU and the United Kingdom market requires that the Commission, in assessing equivalence, be particularly mindful of the risks for the EU in terms of financial stability, market transparency, market integrity, investor protection and level-playing field. In addition, the United Kingdom government's stated intention to diverge from the Union's regulatory and supervisory frameworks in the area of financial services after the transition period requires that the Commission assess UK equivalence in each area on a forward-looking basis"* [**EU Policy Paper 2020** (July 2020)].

The Perspective: Selective Equivalence Policy

The process is therefore complex, but there is no doubt that – once the deal on goods and services is completed – the parties will be mutually interested in reaching an agreement on financial services.

EU-related business accounts for one third of the business in the City of London and obviously European companies will not want to lose access to the City's *deep and liquid market.*

There is also a mutual interest in avoiding disruptions to ordinary business and providing some form of continuity to the regulatory framework. The **Trade and Cooperation Agreement** does not go beyond an attached "***Joint Declaration*** *on Financial Services Regulatory Cooperation*" containing only two articles, confirming the commitment to shared objectives (*financial stability, market integrity*, and *the* *protection of investors and consumers*) as the only mutual recognition.

The *Joint Declaration* also confirms the willingness of the Parties

> *"to establish structured regulatory cooperation (…) between autonomous jurisdictions"* (art. 1).

The "framework for this cooperation" will be based on *"equivalence determinations* (…) *without prejudice to the unilateral and autonomous decision-making process of each side"* (Art. 2).

"Unilateral" and "autonomous" **equivalence determinations** will start from the recognition that the new "third party's" legislation is substantially aligned with EU financial regulation. This is the basis for the future partnership, although it may prove fragile in the case of a UK initiative (immediately or not) to deviate from the *single rulebook*.

This last aspect is particularly delicate, as the "equivalence" regime is periodically reviewed and a first favourable decision can be revoked – unless there is almost automatic implementation of new EU regulation initiatives – at short notice, even only 30 days.

However, the importance of the equivalence regime may vary according to the different categories of financial services based in London.

To give an account:

- *capital markets* are based on the ability of issuers to access investors and trade their securities in global markets. Therefore, there will be no significant impact in terms of liquidity issues or funding costs;
- *hedging services* deal with derivative trading assets and are also managed on a global scale;
- *investment banks* – instead, have an overall role in facilitating European companies' debt and equity raising, and would incur a serious impact. However, these are primarily US based banks and there are virtually no significant UK investment banks left.
- *commercial banking* will be totally excluded from any direct access to the EU: the "equivalence" regime does not in itself cover lending services of third country banks, not even the operation of payment systems;
- *brokerage underwriting, M&A, advisory, and trading* are activities that could be included in the equivalence regime.

On the basis of the above categories, a realistic prospective mutual solution may consider the **selective equivalence regime** as a **regulatory option**. This approach could lead to the development of a regime applicable to those activities mentioned above that are more suitable for an equivalence regime. This would safeguard autonomous regulatory areas especially for investment banks where the EU regulatory apparatus (as for the *Markets In Financial Instruments Directive*, MIFID II *Directive* 2014/56/EU in the relationship with customers) can be a source of "contentious case" between the parties, interfering significantly in the equivalence decisions process.

The EU Commission adopted a prudential and gradual approach on 21 September 2020 allowing EU based banks to continue to access UK clearing houses (the derivative clearing market is completely dominated by the City) until mid-2022. This is to prepare the market infrastructure to move business back to the EU as part of the process of not being overly dependent on a "*third country*" for financial services.

In any case, equivalence determinations provide EU authorities with the opportunity to couple with *reciprocity*, and to seek concessions in return, such as authorisation procedures, investor protection and enforcement capabilities.

As is well known, the issue is likely to create tensions, but a high level of divergence is neither sustainable nor desirable. In the longer term, equivalence will be seen with deep distrust – both inside and outside the EU – if it is too closely associated with an exercise of power aimed at strict adherence of the UK financial system to EU regulations. This in the assumption that

> *"if the UK wanted to benefit from the EU equivalence regime in the future, it would need to follow the evolutions of European financial regulation and become a European regulation taker"* [T. PHILIPPONAT, in J. ARMOUR, H. EIDENMÜLLER (2017)].

Conversely, the *"structured regulatory cooperation"* envisaged by the *Joint Declaration* will only realize its potential if the Parties develop a more robust and reciprocal approach, resulting in a demand for rules that are proportionate, cost-effective and suited to the specific purpose of equivalent regimes.

Part 3

POLICY

Competing in Global Economies

Chapter 7
SOVEREIGNTY

"If this is so, and we do nothing, what then?
Why, we shall, to use the vulgar expression,
be "left out in the cold" [...]
Before long all Europe, save England,
will have one money, and England will be left
outstanding with another money"
(WALTER BAGEHOT, 1866)

Monetary Policy and Plural Institutional Systems

The epigraph of this chapter recalls a warning that The Economist's editor issued when various exchange rate regimes emerged in Europe in the 19th century, including the Latin Monetary Union (LMU), established in 1865, which embraced Belgium, France, Italy, and Switzerland. In the end the LMU collapsed, but today these words sound like an echo of the past.

In contemporary times there has always been tension between the aspiration for a "closer Union" of the EU and the reality of Economic and Monetary Union (EMU) membership. While in principle, all EU Member States were expected to join the EMU as soon as they qualified for membership – i.e., as soon as they complied with the convergence criteria – in practice things have been different from the beginning. In fact, two Member States, the UK and Denmark, negotiated an "opt-out" status which has been included in the treaties. In general, there is no longer the expectation that EU membership implies the aspiration to participate in the Eurozone.

Most of the UK's "reluctant" membership was dedicated to negotiating and obtaining opt-outs and special clauses. Emblematic of this unique relationship is the fact that the UK secured several opt-outs in three areas that are central to the ***concept of sovereignty****:*

- *The first is monetary union. By extension, the UK did not participate in other forms of closer integration of the Eurozone;*
- *The second opt-out concerned the Schengen Agreement, which abolished border controls in some Member States;*
- *The third opt-out concerned justice and home affairs.*

For such reasons, the UK's status has been constantly defined as a "permanent outsider":

> *"over the intervening period, the UK was able to retain more control over its policy domain than any other Member State, save Denmark through the systematic use of opt-outs"* [or what international relations literature calls] *"'outsiderness': draw a line* [...] *and establish an area where they are to remain sovereign"* [K. NICOLAÏDIS, in F. FABBRINI (2017)].

A questionable definition, in the light of interactions even with the Eurozone, i.e. in an area where the UK's ***outsiderness*** *would apparently exclude any reciprocity of* ***influence****.*

In any case the effect of all the opt-outs (also extended to the "social" pillars of EU policy) has been to create the ***institutional dualism*** *of* ***policies.***

The emergence, through the single currency and related issues, of differentiation between a ***"Constitution économique"*** *that included the EU-28 countries and a* ***"Constitution monétaire"*** *for the EU-19 (with the UK being– at the time – the most relevant of the* ***outs****), has given rise to* ***plural institutional systems*** **(EU and EMU)**.

It is significant – at present – that while the UK 'opt out' of the single currency has been not unique, being common to eight other countries, it was by far the most important historically, culturally, and economically. In other words, the choice made by the "Treasury" had the striking and undeniable effect of being the ***cause*** *and the* ***starting point*** *of the EMU as a (largely) autonomous institutional system.*

On the other hand, institutions in a democratic society are not legitimated by claims of abstract validity. The analysis of solutions offered by a given market economy in a given period of time should avoid any preconception.

What needs to be explored is the extent to which legal solutions, implemented from time to time, correspond to the structures and the propensities of a given economy at that time. By now, the EU and the UK – within the framework of the "new partnership" – will deploy

competing policies *in monetary areas, fiscal* ***governance*** *(infra Ch. 8) and* ***global*** *trade (infra Ch. 9).*

Currency and Sovereignty

The right to mint coin is a privilege of **sovereignty**. Historically the state (and politically the crown or the executive) had the power to create and circulate coins.

In the modern era the adoption of a **currency not issued by a state** took place for the first time with the euro: the process of creating the new currency – and the corresponding changeover of (initially) eleven different national currencies – was the result of the transfer of sovereignty to the **institutions** exercising this right at the **supranational level**.

The transfer of currency powers from nation states to a supranational institution, which authorized the issuance of a currency resulting from the convergence process, is the result of an evolution over time. A few centuries ago, monetary integration was complete, and not merely in Europe.

> *"All countries shared the same money – gold – so that the world formed a sort of monetary union but in a different world. There was no central bank as we know them and no monetary policy. The discovery of paper money changed all that"* [R. BALDWIN, C. WYPLOSZ (2019)].

In European monetary history, paper money was already circulating among medieval merchants, but the **invention** of the banknote in the modern sense of the term is attributed to the banker Johan Palmstruch, director of the Swedish Stockholm's Banco, who was of Dutch origin and began using it around 1656.

> *"Stockholms Banco was a deposit bank which also lent money to the public. The loans and deposit receipts were issued in banknotes, which were claims on the bank. The banknotes were standardized like modern paper notes and were preferred to the heavy copper plates used in Sweden as a means of payment at the time"* [K.G. PERSSON, P. SHARP (2015)].

Although this invention belongs to a Nordic country, it was the intelligent and persistent action of the **Bank of England** which, at the end of the 17th century, fostered its use in the main financial centres in deciding the fortunes of the banknote:

> *"England became the pioneer in developing note-issuing banks during the 1690s and into the eighteenth century. Banks in London, and later in the century throughout England and Scotland, offered deposit facilities, discounting, clearing and note-issuing: most notably through the Bank of England, founded in 1694, but also through a number of local banks"* [*Ibid*].

This was the origin of "fiduciary" money. *Fiducia,* a *latin* word for "trust", implies a "public" commitment. Thus, when paper money was initially poorly understood, the emergence of *fiduciary money* – once again – was due to the role played by an **English institution**:

> *"Gradually, by protracted process of trial and error, the Bank of England developed public functions, in return for the reaffirmation of its monopoly on note issue in 1826"* [N. FERGUSON (2008)].

A Stateless Supranational Currency

In modern times the Bretton Woods system, created in 1944, offered *exchange rate stability*.

Plans for a *monetary union* in Europe, formally proposed by the European Commission beginning in 1962, were supported by Willy Brandt, the then German chancellor.

The plan was taken up in the 1971 Werner Report, named after the Luxembourg prime minister. This report, in support of the adoption of a **single currency,** was approved in 1972 by all European heads of government including those of the three countries that had planned to join the club in 1973: Denmark, Ireland and the United Kingdom. Indeed, at a summit held in Paris in December 1972 with the heads of state, all nine national leaders including Britain's Edward Heath signed to pursue not only **monetary union,** but also **political union** by 1980.

The project was disrupted by external factors, such as, *inter alia,* the global recession of the early 1970s.

European political leaders (Valery Giscard d'Estaing, Helmut Schmidt, and Roy Jenkins) devised – as a replacement – the creation of a fixed system of exchange rates in the form of the *European Monetary System* (EMS). In March 1979 the EMS was established. The heart of the EMS was the *Exchange Rate Mechanism*, a system of fixed and adjustable exchange rates managed jointly and backed by mutual support. It took the form of an explicitly asymmetric arrangement with no currency at its centre.

As is well known, the system failed because of the speculative attacks on currencies (in particular on the British and Italian national currencies) in 1992, the success of which was due to the absence of a common institution capable of supporting the fixed rate exchange.

Meanwhile, a second attempt to create a single currency began in the 1980s.

> *"Tommaso Padoa-Schioppa was the intellectual force behind the creation of the euro, providing the economic argument to bolster the political case for monetary union. [...] Padoa-Schioppa said that by creating a single currency and a European Central Bank it would be possible for Europe to have free trade within its own borders, free movement of capital and a fixed exchange rate. In return, they would have to give up control of their own monetary policy. Padoa-Schioppa's arguments helped shape the Delors Report of 1989, which in turn led to the Maastricht Treaty of 1991"* [L. ELLIOT, D. ATKINSON (2016)].

The Delors Report, commissioned by the European Council, was followed by two intergovernmental conferences, the conclusions of which were presented to the Maastricht European Council. It took almost a decade to achieve monetary union, ascertaining the existence of elements connecting **a single currency** with **a certain legal system.**

According to the regulatory provisions, the single currency required access conditions – i.e. the *convergence criteria* – which were largely laid down at the request of Germany. The latter, which considered the strong *Deutschmark* an essential achievement and a key factor for economic success, was not willing to exchange it for a weaker currency. After the fall of the Berlin wall, Chancellor Helmut Kohl accepted the idea of giving up the Deutschmark as the price for unification. For its part, France favoured a new single currency, largely to compensate for the growing power of a new united Germany.

Compliance with the convergence criteria was assessed at the end of 1997 (paradoxically under the British presidency of the European Union). Eventually, thanks in part to window-dressing and creative accounting, all EU Member States that wanted to adopt the euro qualified.

Precedents in History

Precedents in the history of monetary unions indicate the need for robust **institutional architecture** for the final survival of the union.

As previously mentioned, in 1865 Belgium, France, Italy and Switzerland and then Greece formed the **Latin Monetary Union (LMU),** a distant ancestor of today's monetary union with the aim of preserving bimetallism. After the Franco-German War of 1870, the newly established German Empire moved from silver to gold and weakened French finances by imposing war reparations to be paid in gold. When silver discoveries depressed the price of silver, the Latin European Monetary Union was abandoned in 1878 and gold became the monetary standard.

Only five years earlier, in 1873, Denmark, Norway and Sweden had created the **Scandinavian Monetary Union (SMU)** as part of the 'Scandinavianism' movement to support the symbol of a common "krona", with their currencies circulating widely in their respective countries. At the outbreak of World War I, the Scandinavian Monetary Union ceased to exist, although it formally survived until 1924:

> *"These precedents are merely of historical interest and bear little resemblance to modern monetary unions now that the currency is no longer metallic and central banks create money. These old monetary unions amounted to nothing more than harmonized coinage. They were not associated with any trade agreement and, more importantly, there was no common central bank and very little coordination among the national monetary authorities. When external conditions became difficult* [...], *each country reacted in its own way to protect its own interests"* [R. BALDWIN, C. WYPLOSZ (2019)].

Successful monetary unions, such as the one between German or American states, survived thanks to subsequent political union and the resulting economic and budgetary union.

Many other examples support this point. The attempt by British colonial administrations in the 20th century to form common currencies for some of the newly independent states was unsuccessful. The collapse of a central power like the Soviet Union led to the birth of independent currencies. The Czechoslovakian currency lasted a few weeks after the country's break-up into two states and the same happened in the case of Ireland and the UK's monetary union which, although it lasted longer after independence, ended with the division of currencies.

Another indirect, albeit hypothetical example would be the issuance of the future currency of a new independent secessionist state.

> *"Before the 2014 referendum, the Scottish Government had declared that, if Scotland became independent, it would like to continue to use the Pound Sterling and to remain in a monetary union with the remainder of the UK. The British authorities had firmly and immediately rejected this prospect. Taking the crisis of the Eurozone as an example not to be followed, they pointed out that a monetary union without a corresponding economic and fiscal (budgetary) union would entail serious risks"* [J.-C. PIRIS, in C. CLOSA (2017)].

The Institutions of the Euro

The euro's institutional system differs from previous attempts at monetary unification in that it combines a single currency and a single central bank, the *European Central Bank*, even though Member States maintain considerable *political* and *fiscal sovereignty*. The problems of the *Economic and Monetary Union* are, in these aspects, those faced by previous monetary unions in terms of *"diverging interests of members"* and consequent *"current account asymmetries"* [M. RYNER, A. CAFRUNY (2017)].

The **institutional framework** remains the central issue in the area of monetary union. According to Nobel prize winner Stiglitz the issue is:

> *"precisely, the creation of a single currency without creating a set of institutions that enabled a region of Europe's diversity to function effectively with a single currency"* [J.E. STIGLITZ (2016)].

This view should be mitigated considering that, unlike the aforementioned examples of the Latin and Scandinavian monetary unions in which there was no central **institutional structure** to fall back on, the **supranational institutional dimension** plays a key role in a modern economic and monetary union. In fact, there is *no previous historical equivalent,* but according to the same author the institutional framework would not be sufficient or adequate:

> *"there needs to be an array of institutions that can help those nations for which the policies are not well suited. Europe failed to create these institutions.* [...] *While the euro was a political project, the political cohesion – especially around the notion of delegation of powers from the sovereign countries to the EU – was not strong enough to create the economic institutions that might have given the euro a chance to succeed"* [*Ibid*].

There has been no lack of criticism in the UK. UK Prime Minister David Cameron, speaking twelve years after the euro began to circulate, stressed that there are a number of features common to all successful currency unions:

> *"the deepest possible economic integration with the flexibility to deal with economic shocks; and a system of fiscal transfers and collective debt issuance that can deal with the tensions and imbalances between different countries and regions within the union. Currently it's not that the euro zone doesn't have all of these; it's that it doesn't really have any of these"* [David Cameron *Speech at Davos in Switzerland*, January 2012, cited by J. Peet, A. La Guardia (2014)].

"Constitution économique" and *"constitution monétaire"*

In fact, twenty years of single currency has not led to a degree of economic integration with the necessary flexibility to deal with economic shocks, nor even to a system of fiscal transfers to deal with imbalances within the Union. Only a new economic **shock** like the one caused by the **pandemic crisis** is now putting **collective debt issuance** on the agenda.

However, the above criticism does not capture the difference with the previous experience. The difference lies in the institutional architecture of the system endowed with powers that have **direct ef-**

fects on all the national economies of the Eurozone, giving rise to a **specific institutional system** within the EU, the EMU.

The latter system has its own institutional architecture entrusted to a completely *new institutional entity*, the *European System of Central Banks* (ESCB), a body composed of national governors of the central banks and the newly created *European Central Bank* (ECB).

The architecture was enriched in 2011 (by an EU Council Decision which was then transposed into an international treaty) with the establishment of the *European Stability Mechanism* (ESM). The ESM acts as a *rescue fund* by releasing credit lines for EMU Member States that would need support in coping with the debt crisis. The *credit lines* are subject to *strong conditionality*, which imply a closely monitored reform programme or fiscal consolidation necessary to restore financial stability. With a *euro area* bailout instrument, the Eurozone was – to some extent – sheltered from the "sovereign debt" crisis of that period.

In order to address the current economic crisis stemming from the **pandemic emergency** that is symmetrically affecting all EU countries, the ESM has become part of a package to mitigate the impact of the economic effects on the euro area, with the possibility of release of *precautionary credit lines* without conditions if resources are exclusively allocated to the health sector [Council of the EU, ***Report*** *on the comprehensive economic policy response to the COVID-19* pandemic (sec. 16), 9 April 2020].

The set of institutions supporting the establishment of an economic and monetary union was in fact the starting point for the creation of two largely different **institutional systems** (the EU and EMU) only partially coinciding as far as the Member States are concerned, but profoundly different in terms of **institutional actors.**

The rules concerning **monetary policy** are directly applicable only in one of the two legal systems, giving rise to *"la Constitution monétaire"*.

The creation of a *stateless currency* is, in other words, an expression of **political choices** establishing **constitutional powers**. The consequences are visible in terms of removing *monetary sovereignty* from states that throughout history have had primary responsibility for this function, conceived of as the core of the state. The effect has been the (partial) removal of state discretionary power in the definition of **economic policy**, as national economic policies have lost the possibility to use the instrument of currency exchange.

Over the years, the EU and the EMU have seen their framework of institutions and rules progressively differentiate among themselves.

Alongside the political and economic effects of any prospective process of deepening integration, what is now clear is the emergence and development, within the same territory of the European Union, of two institutional systems differentiating a ***constitution économique*** for the EU-27 from a ***constitution monétaire*** for the EU-19. The concept of overlapping systems is shared by legal theorists:

> *"The idea of two or more legal orders existing within the same society or territory is neither novel nor problematic"* [D.J. GALLIGAN (2007)].

Contemporary institutional systems offer several examples of overlapping jurisdictions, segmented authorities and multiple loyalties. The multiplicity of supranational systems leads to a *"heterarchical"* rather than a "*hierarchical*" model:

> *"Many theorists now believe legal pluralism, which describes a state of affairs in which two or more legal orders occupy the same legal space, to be the most convincing theory of law"* [S. DOUGLAS-SCOTT, in R. SCHÜTZE *et al.* (2018)].

Following the above definition, the EU and the EMU constitute two **institutional systems** occupying the same partly overlapping legal space. The economic constitution has taken on a new dimension: l'*ordre monétaire.*

Consequently, by creating its own institutions for the implementation of monetary policy, EMU constitutes *"un sous-ordre au sous-système de l'ordre juridique de l'Union"* [F. MARTUCCI, in G. KALFLÈCHE *et al.* (2018)], operating in some way as a *separate institutional system* occupying the same space (albeit more limited) in the EU legal order.

Leadership in the Monetary System

On the other hand, the UK's choice of opting **out** of the common currency has produced historical implications.

Since 1914, Britain's traditional leadership in international monetary matters has been undermined by the growing challenge of the United States. The UK decided to return to its pre-war gold parity, *to look the dollar in the face*. As a result, prices rose much more in the UK than in the newly emerging economic power, i.e. the United States. Historically, it was the product of a

> *"religion of financial orthodoxy whose Trinity was Free Trade, Balanced Budgets and the Gold Standard, whose Original Sin was the National Debt* [...]. *The cult, which obsessed successive generations in the nineteenth century, died sometime between the two World Wars"* [H. ROSEVEARE (1969)].

Finally, the Bank of England withdrew from the gold standard in 1931, recognizing that an ambition of the past was no longer justified in contemporary times.

The creation of the single currency has once again raised issues deriving from *past political and economic leadership* in the *global monetary system*.

> *"The deepest political consequence of the euro's creation, at least for the United Kingdom, is that it spelt the end of centuries of British foreign policy aimed at maintaining a balance of power in Europe.* [...] *When most of western Europe proved willing to pool sovereignty by giving up their national currencies for the euro, it was going to create a community of interests that the United Kingdom could never hope to counterbalance"* [M. SANDBU (2015)].

At the beginning of the new millennium there was a real debate about the potential accession of the United Kingdom to the Eurozone. The **loss of sovereignty** implicit in the single currency was considered – at least in principle – consistent with Britain's economic interest. In Tony Blair's words in 1997:

> *"In an era of sweeping globalization, European monetary union will provide an essential foundation for stable and sustainable growth that generates jobs. A single European currency will weaken the power of those who thrive on monetary chaos and financial speculation"* [cited by L. ELLIOT, D. ATKINSON (2016)].

The real choice for Britain in Europe came at that time:

"the creation of the euro left the United Kingdom with just one choice: between resigning itself to marginalisation or joining the eurozone". [M. SANDBU (2015)]

The assumptions of the intimate connection between monetary and fiscal policies underline the *British approach*:

"The British approach was the consequence of a long history of being apart from European dynamics but also from a central paradox of political economy: the recognition (following the basic lines of the Anglo-American approach) that monetary unions need fiscal unions to work, but at the same time a profound conviction that Great Britain did not want to participate in further European integration." [M.K. BRUNNERMEIER *et al.* (2016)].

The choice was political but had a precise constitutional background:

"two elements of the new structure were particularly foreign to traditional UK constitutional arrangements. The first was their essentially federal character, evident in the ESCB itself and in the representation of the governors of national central banks in the governing council of the ECB. The second major characteristic was the establishment of a strong normative framework for monetary policy in the Treaty rather than relying only on political direction and supervision" [T. PROSSER (2014)].

The risk for *non-euro* Member States is however that they are **marginalized** in the fundamental **decision-making** relating directly or indirectly to the euro and the risk is emphasized by the clear fact that euro area Member States form a single block in the Council's decision-making process.

"Marginalisation can have several negative consequences for outs", e.g. *"negative spillover effects of euro area decisions, domination by euro area interests over the non-euro area"* [T. BEUKERS, B. de WITTE, C. KILPATRICK, in T. BEUKERS *et al.* (2017)].

The Currency Choice: the "Five tests"

Although the theoretical premises were clearly in place, the UK Government – at the beginning of the effective circulation of the single currency (2002) – announced that the verdict on joining the euro would be based on five economic and financial tests (i.e. *convergence, flexibility, investment, financial services, growth, stability* and *employment*).

The Treasury report determined that only two of the five tests – "investment" and "financial" (relating to the **benefits for the City**) – proved positive. The report (*UK Membership of the Single Currency: An Assessment of the Five Economic Tests),* published in June 2003, also found that the United Kingdom was more aligned with the Eurozone than some euro-members in the run-up to the launch of monetary union in 1999 and *"remains more convergent than a number of EMU countries today"*.

Although the issue of Britain's accession to the Eurozone generated strong opinions, the Treasury's assessment was based on the best analysis that the macroeconomics of the time could provide.

Historians had already observed that a *"history of Treasury could hardly fall short of being at the same time a social, an economic and a political history of Britain"* [H. ROSEVEARE (1969)] and that the *"foundations of control"* were vested in the Treasury as

> *"a distinct administrative entity with a permanent and well-defined presence in the machinery of English government"* and *"the dominant arbiter of financial administration"* developing *"a comprehensive and quite radical philosophy of the public interest"* [H. ROSEVEARE (1973)].

In performing its role:

> *"It takes responsibility for the government as a whole and acts as if it-were more than a repository of a single minister's domain"* [H. HECLO, A. WILDAVSKY (1974)].

As already said, in the political and economic debate, the original five tests were overcome by the belief that a monetary union cannot work economically without a **fiscal union**, and that a fiscal union is **politically impossible** without a **political union**. This became an undisputed axiom in the British political debate.

Since both fiscal union and political union were unacceptable to the majority of the British people (as subsequently demonstrated in the 2016 referendum), monetary union was also excluded.

The recognition of this outsiderness was enshrined in the statute of the ECB:

> *"the United Kingdom shall retain its powers in the field of monetary policy according to national law' and the Statute of the ESCB states that central banks of countries with a derogation shall retain their powers in the field of monetary policy according to national law".*

The Basic Eurozone Norm

The distinction between the EMU and the EU is the effect of different **constitutional and institutional** features.

Without broaching the field of legal theory for the definition of a legal system, it is sufficient to consider – to this end – that the EMU is managed according to *"legal rules emanating from the same sovereign will"* [J.W. HARRIS (1979)].

The positive legal rules are given by its own *institutional system* (the "*sovereign will*"), which applies only to Member States that adopt the euro:

> *"The first way in which way the euro area has grown further apart from non-euro countries is through the adoption of special EU legislation that applies only to euro countries"* [A. HINAREJOS (2015)].

From this perspective, Article 136(1) TFEU, which allows the Council to adopt measures that apply **only to euro area members**, can be considered – to put it on a more theoretical level – the *"basic norm, the Grundnorm – a grand, indispensable postulate"* [C.K. ALLEN(1964)] of the EU special regime for the euro area.

It is the institutional system that:

a) regulates and provides for preventive budgetary discipline (the *Excessive Deficit Procedure* and the *Macroeconomic Imbalance Procedure)*; and
b) regulates the *common budget* and empowers the Commission to request changes to draft budgets at any time, establishing the *Economic Partnership Programmes;* combining fiscal and structural reforms in euro states when the Council declares an excessive deficit.

The convergence of all the elements that define an "institutional system" suggests that EMU is not merely a paradigm of differentiated integration (as conventionally considered). Nor can it be considered a "federal" legal order. The originality of such a normative framework suggests that the traditional formula of the "federal core" of Europe should not be used, but it should be taken as it is: **a constitutional institutional system.**

Dominant Eurosystem Institutions

The EMU as such, therefore, is not made up exclusively of policies but of *stable institutions* that give life to the characteristics of an *institutional complex.*

The single currency has this peculiarity: unlike the competition sector, whose authorities (the *European Competition Network* and the *Commission*) are absolutely internal to the EU legal order, the single currency creates its own **institutions**. Taking into account the characteristic components of a legal system – *rules and institutions* – both define the EMU.

The **Eurogroup** (made up of the finance ministries of the Eurozone countries) is now at the top of the EMU without interference from other EU institutions. It answers neither to the European Parliament nor to the European Union Court of Justice.

> *"As early as 1998 when the transition of the first Member States to the single currency became imminent, the finance ministers of the new Eurozone created their own informal meeting format with the explicit aim to exclude the British not only from voting but also from ministerial deliberations altogether. Ever since then the so-called Eurogroup has been at the centre of Eurozone economic governance. It is one of the most frequently convened and most influential ministerial groupings in EU governance. It received formal recognition through the Lisbon Treaty"* [U. PUETTER, in F. FABBRINI (2017)].

An autonomous monetary system focuses on a **dominant institution**, which is responsible for monetary policy (setting Eurozone interest rates and controlling euro supply) and for *banking supervision* of the most significant banks in EMU (in this case through a largely autonomous unit, the *Single Supervisory Mechanism*, SSM, *supra* Ch. 6).

On 4 January 1999 the power to conduct *monetary policy* was transferred from each euro area Member State to the *European System of Central Banks* (ESCB). While the latter is composed of the ECB and the national central banks of the EU Member States, its governing council is instead composed of the governors of the central banks of the Eurozone members (*Eurosystem*) and the six members of the ECB's *Executive Board.*

The fundamental value of this evolution is clearly expressed in the **stability** of the currency, seen as a *public good.* Throughout the 20th century, the *national central banks* have protected this value as a public good in a continuous effort to balance it with the financial spending needs of governments.

The supranational central bank was structured with the same aim of ***autonomy*** required by monetary policy to prevent governments from creating currency to finance easy spending. This autonomy is based on the principle that those who create money should not depend on those who spend it.

Important provisions therefore concern the **independence** of the central bank: Article 130 TFEU states that neither the ECB nor the national central banks shall seek or take instructions from the Union's institutions, governments of Member States or any other body. According to Article 131, Member States must ensure that their national legislation is compatible with this principle. Similar provisions are laid down in the ECB's statute.

In the constitutional framework of the EMU and the EU, the ECB's functions appear to differ.

As the EMU's dominant institution, its specific activity relating exclusively to the Eurozone concerns assistance in the form of sovereign debt lending with the provision of *emergency liquidity assistance* (ELA) to euro area banks and euro area debt *bond purchase programmes*, or *quantitative easing* (QE).

On this basis, the ECB's currency stability policy takes absolute precedence over the EU's general economic policies which require monetary policy to play a supportive role for economic and employment growth and the development of a fair and inclusive society. The ECB's priorities in achieving the balance between monetary and economic policies are laid down in the Treaties (Article 119 TFEU):

> *"concurrently [....] these activities shall include a single currency, the euro, and the definition and conduct of a single monetary policy and*

> *exchange-rate policy the primary objective of both of which shall be to maintain price stability and, without prejudice to this objective, to support the general economic policies in the Union, in accordance with the principle of an open market economy with free competition".*

In practice, the ECB has played a central role in the transformation of monetary governance in the second decade of the century, a role defined as "*deliberative supranationalism*", a deliberative process that is not without internal complexity:

> *"the ECB temporarily filled a dangerous governance vacuum by announcing and partly implementing several sovereign debt purchasing programmes. But conflict about the distribution of risks even affected deliberations inside the bank"* [H. DETERS, in C. JORGES, C. GLINSKI (2017)].

While this denotes a deliberative process with full legitimacy ultimately relying on the ECB's role as *lender of last resort to governments*, this role is not permitted by the constitutional provisions of the Treaties (Article 136 TFEU).

Although the principle is not controversial, the recurrent QE programmes appear to be increasingly permanent, allowing the ECB – with all technical differences– to follow a function similar to monetary financing (*infra* Ch. 8).

The Pandemic Emergency and Unconventional Monetary Policy

Due to the effects of recurring economic shocks – including the most recent one caused by the pandemic that gave rise to the *Pandemic Emergency Purchase Programme* (PEPP) – the ECB has reinvented itself, reinterpreting its **mission** in terms of stability and irreversibility of the euro. In this way, the ECB has rewritten the rules and parameters of the central bank function by introducing long-term refinancing operations.

In current times, in order to prevent a global health crisis from turning into a new sovereign debt crisis in the Eurozone (as in the previous decade), the ECB has relaxed many of the restrictions on **bond purchases** (such as the obligation to purchase in proportion to each country's contribution to capital or the requirement to purchase government bonds according to investment grade rank). It has also rethought its role as a central bank with an *unconventional monetary policy*, increasing the instruments at its disposal and bringing more flexibility to its "price stability" mandate.

All this confirms a central assumption, that the ECB is the **only European institution** accustomed to acting **strategically** for the euro area as a whole, partly overcoming the main flaw of the euro's institutional design, i.e. the biggest missing element: *debt mutualisation*.

As mentioned, the impact of the pandemic on the EU economy and public finances is going to give place to the issuance of common debt through *innovative financial instruments* in principle approved by the EU Council [**EU Council Report on 23 April 2020**] and detailed in a subsequent Special Meeting [**EU Council Special Meeting – 22-26 July 2020**]. This will represent a huge innovation in fiscal *governance* (*infra* Ch. 8).

It is also further confirmation of the need to consider the *institutions* as an expression of *choices* that, once established, are forced to change with the *challenges* and *demands of the market economy* over time.

In other words, monetary union is not an exchange system, but rather an ***institutional system*** characterized by the transition from a plurality of decision-making centres for monetary policy to a *single institution* taking responsibility for a single monetary system.

The potential completion of the EMU's institutional system is currently the subject of political debate.

Although some elements of the governance regime are shared between the EU and the EMU (such as the *Fiscal Compact*, the multilevel budgetary process, and the European Semester), it is correct to say that the EMU's

> *"institutional mechanism and decision-making rules are now well settled, and there are no signs indicating that it will soon be absorbed into mainstream EU law"* [T. BEUKERS, B. de WITTE, C. KILPATRICK (2017)].

The EMU has a proper constitutional structure. Given that in economic terms *"constitutions are concerned with mechanisms for the production of public goods"* and the single currency itself is determined to produce the maximum amount of public goods, it can be said that it gives rise to a *"de facto constitution"* [S. VOIGT, in F. PARISI (2017)]. The result is a *"Union reinforce* [...] *au niveau de la zone euro"* and *"la pluralité constitutive de l'Europe"* [A. MINC (2019)], a way to define the concept of plural legal systems applying to the same territory.

In other words, pluralism will continue to be a *permanent feature* of the **European institutional landscape**, characterized by *two institutional systems (partly) occupying the same space.*

The ECB under German Constitutional Court Scrutiny

The picture of euro-law, despite the UK's absence from the EMU legal system, changes significantly in the medium-term perspective with the UK's exit from the EU.

What is at stake is the *balance* between the EU and EMU. Since the UK has been the most influential non-euro country, it may be plausible that the *centralized debt issuance* by the Commission will result in a diminished role for non-euro countries, being in itself a step toward "*financial risk-sharing*" and thus **financial integration**. The event may lead to greater homogeneity of domestic law within the EU-EMU institutional systems.

So far, the euro, a *stateless currency*, has not produced a push towards deeper political integration (two decades have shown no signs in this direction), but rather has set up a proper system with a specific *constitutional formulation* given by the total transfer of *sovereignty* in the monetary and banking areas.

Unlike the EU, a Member State cannot leave the *Economic Monetary Union* without broad social and political implications, and, furthermore, there is no formal procedure to trigger withdrawal on the basis of the Treaties.

Therefore, on the one hand it is correct to agree that the creation of the euro

> *"was and continues to be an ambitious and unique experiment, because it involves a shared currency being used by a group of countries that have retained sovereignty over their political and fiscal systems and their own economic responsibilities. This is why the single currency would not have been possible if it had not been seen right from the start as part of a more ambitious project of political integration"* [L. RECHLIN, in G. AMATO *et al.* (2018)].

On the other hand, the failure to pursue the path of political integration has led to a **network of contradictions** among the Member States, obscuring prospects for the stability of the project.

The incompleteness of the euro's architecture – its dependence on *"a technocracy of governing: power without the state"* [C. JORGES, C. GLINSKI (2017)] – is, therefore, something that goes beyond the existing technical problems of *risk-sharing* rules among Member States.

It will be deeply vulnerable until the existing **constitutional legitimacy** of the institutions protecting such architectures is fully defined.

At present, when monetary policy gives rise to conflicts rooted in **national interest**, the emergence of **national constitutional identity** undermines the very foundations of the EMU legal system. The recent ruling of the German Constitutional Court (*BVerfG*, Judgment of the Second Senate of 5 May 2020) as already mentioned (*supra, Introduction*), raises conflicts between the CJEU and a national constitutional court in the hierarchy of the Treaties' judicial sources. Furthermore, it assumes that a national court has the competence to examine and decide on the question of the ECB's compliance with the Treaties. By examining the constitutional complaints against the ECB's decisions on the *Public Sector Purchase Programme* (PSPP), the *BVerfG*'s ruling states:

> *"In the decisions at issue, the ECB fails to conduct the necessary balancing of the monetary policy objective against the economic policy effects arising from the programme. Therefore, the decisions at issue violate Art. 5(1) second sentence and Art. 5/4) TEU and, in consequence, exceed the monetary policy mandate of the ECB".*

It is a direct *vulnus* to the ECB mandate to argue that the acts of the ECB's Governing Council *"must be qualified as ultra vires acts, despite the CJEU's judgment to the contrary".*

This reasoning implies the assumption that the ECB – a supranational institution whose statutory limits are defined at a supranational level in terms of independence from Member States' national institutions – is instead subject to the scrutiny of a national court. The consequences are the same even if the immediate effect of the ruling is formally directed at the *Bundesbank*, evoking a scenario in which the German Central Bank *"may thus no longer participate in the implementation and execution of the ECB decisions at issue"*. The interference with the autonomy of the ECB's biggest shareholder is further accentuated by the indirect conditioning impact on the ordinary functioning of the ESCB Governing Council to the extent that the ECB *"will, in the long run, hold fewer assets on its balance sheet as a consequence of this ruling"*

[W. MÜNCHAU, *"The European Central Bank is deluding itself over German court ruling"*, in *Financial Times*, 10 May 2020].

Apart from this specific issue, the overall effect of the *BVerfG* ruling is only a plastic demonstration of the **vulnerability** of the constitutional legitimacy of the EMU institutions. This is despite the fact that the Treaties expressly state that not only the ECB, but not even *"a national central bank"* shall seek instructions *"from any government of a Member State or* [to be noted] *from any other body"* [TFEU, Protocol No 4, Ch. III, Article 7].

This is not the sole aspect on which – as pointed out– EMU Member States must seek to *"realign interests"* [M. CHANG (2004)] among themselves.

Currency Power and Institutional Architecture

The most disturbing aspect of the Eurozone is that the divergence of economic interests makes it even more difficult for a common currency to work for the benefit of all, pursuing

> *"a shared sense of common destiny that outweighs the nationalist tendencies that would otherwise call for intransigent reactions"* [R. BALDWIN, C. WYPLOSZ (2019)].

The fundamental political problem for a single currency to work in an area with enormous economic, political and social diversity is the disjunction between responsibility for *monetary policy* and *national political accountability* for *economic policy*. An issue (and a challenge) with deep theoretical implications, defying the limits of the ordo-liberalism doctrine:

> *"les idées de l'ordo-libéralisme reviennent au premier plan et se heurtent aux besoin pratiques de la construction de la nouvelle monnaie commune"* [G. KALFLECHE, *et al.* (2018)].

While living in a monetary union should increase the sense of common destiny among sovereign countries, as suggested by the depth and breadth of the *"single currency power"* [B.J. COHEN (2015)], asymmetry within the fiscal policy framework (*infra*, Ch. 8)

> *"brought about unintended consequences in economic policy as it contributed to the widening divergence of euro area economies"* [M. CHANG (2016)].

Countries forming a currency area should take into account the impact of asymmetric economic shocks:

> *"When separate countries contemplate the formation of a currency area, they need to realize that there will be times when disagreements will occur and that these disagreements may follow national lines, especially if the shocks are asymmetric or produce asymmetric effects. For such disagreements to be manageable, the people who form the currency union must accept mutual concessions. This will come easily when they share a sense of solidarity"* [R. BALDWIN, C. WYPLOSZ (2019)].

On a strictly monetary level, since its inception and actual circulation, the euro has become the second most widely used currency in the world (although still much less than the dollar in terms of global foreign exchange and reserves, as it is undermined by the fragmentation of private securities markets and a few governments issuing triple-A-rated bonds).

However, the **currency's power** is now well defined, with the role of the euro as an instrument to defend the interests of the euro area in terms of *industrial* and *trade policy*:

> *"a more prominent euro is key to securing the region's financial and monetary autonomy"* [and protecting the region from the dollar's] *"exorbitant privilege"*, e.g. *"the dollar's prominence that put Europe at commercial disadvantage and helped provide the Europeans' motivations on the long road to monetary union"* [M. SANDBU, *Taking on the greenback,* in *Financial Times*, 5 December 2019].

It is a path that – if pursued – will lead to the strengthening of its **institutional architecture**, a necessary condition not only for the proper functioning of a currency area, but also for something more: a necessary condition for *overcoming nationalist tendencies* potentially capable of jeopardising an *original* and *powerful construction*.

Chapter 8
GOVERNANCE

"We must remain,
as we have always been in the past,
different in character from other European
nations and fundamentally incapable
of wholehearted integration with them"
(ERNEST BEVIN, 1949)

Fiscal Policy and Common Debt Instruments

It is certain that – according to the vision of then Foreign Secretary Ernest Bevin – ***wholehearted integration*** *is exactly what has been lacking in the membership years and not only from the side of the United Kingdom.*

> *"A full economic and fiscal union would require a high degree of financial solidarity, in that such a union would most likely encompass some sort of transfer or automatic equalization mechanism between euro members"* [A. HINAREJOS (2015)].

This, in turn, would require a high degree of ***political solidarity****, which seemed – at least until recently - quite unattainable given that European nations are under the pressure of* ***defensive nationalism****, certainly less aggressively than in the past, but it has not helped to forge the financial solidarity that is needed.*

The issue is critical because it is here, in the area of fiscal and economic policy, that the matter of ***distribution policy*** *becomes relevant. This happens when the issues of competitive economy interact with those of* ***equity****. Thanks to redistribution policies, the first allocations of resources change as a result of fiscal policies.*

Consequently, "distribution" issues require some basis of substantial ***legitimacy****. When redistribution issues prevail, the legitimacy of choices* *can only be guaranteed by systems of majority* ***representation*** *that lead to direct* ***political accountability****.*

In particular, different strategies to solve a situation involving high indebtedness have different consequences in terms of redistribution among social groups, often with conflicting economic interests in the policies to be pursued. The specific interests and political strength of the various target groups can heavily weigh on governments' choices in dealing with high public debt.

Distributive justice is in itself ***procedural justice****. The agreement behind the* ***veil of ignorance*** *concerns the "just division of social advantages": "a doctrine of political economy must include an interpretation of the public good which is based on a conception of justice" J. RAWLS [1971]. This conception cannot concern the merits of choices in income distribution, but rather the* ***rules*** *of how to proceed in making choices. The conditioning values here are only those with constitutional force.*

Solidarity and Asymmetries

One of the main obstacles so far in adopting the **solidarity mechanisms** mentioned above has been the difficulty of justifying them to citizens on the basis of an assumed "European identity".

Obviously, even the citizens of a given state are not entirely homogeneous in their values. However, they share a certain understanding of the mechanism for redistributing resources within the state on the basis of "national identity".

In another context, like the European Union and also in the European Monetary Union, national societies do not share a **common identity** or an awareness of their interdependence as it would be if they were fully committed to organic solidarity.

The overall picture is characterized by significant global contradictions.

In recent decades, obstacles to the implementation of shared economic policies have been identified. In fact, the process of economic globalization produced by the progressive liberalization of trade in goods and capital changed the very concept of the state. As a result, among other things, **policies** have moved increasingly outside national political and administrative powers: world trade is regulated more by international organizations than by states (**multilateral insti-**

tutions around the world including the WTO, the IMF, the World Bank, the G8 and G20, and regional organizations such as NAFTA, MERCOSUR, and ASEAN, are all institutions designed for the *global market and global governance*) and political decisions often go beyond national competences.

The reduced institutional role of the territory makes state **policies** dependent on **market** assessments.

Furthermore, some Member States operate as economic areas which, although part of the Union, are in effect – at tax level – offshore centres.

In general, the current configuration of international economic relations is unprecedented. Never before has there been such a *high degree of capital mobility, large global markets* and *flexible exchange rates* between major currencies and *deeply-rooted integration* of economies associated with the pure fiat currency.

These are just some of the **asymmetries** between problems and solutions at a time when globalization is clashing with the fact that **state authority is not global** and the balance between the power of financial markets and the *rule of law* is one of the current challenges.

The *EU Recovery Fund* (NGEU) will represent, also in this respect, a reference point that combines a political and legal commitment (as shown by the link between the common funding and a mechanism that makes the disbursement of funds conditional on the respect of "**rule of law**" by the Member States after the dispute with Hungary and Poland (European Parliament, *Resolution of 17 December 2020 on the Multiannual Financial Framework 2021-2027,* **The EU Recovery Instrument and the Rule of Law Regulation**).

On the other hand – paradoxically – *national borders* count today as they did in the past because they cannot be physically crossed as easily as financial capital, thus from an economic, social and political point of view determining crucial factors in terms of opportunities for individuals and companies.

Economic Stabilisation Policy

In the absence of public bodies corresponding to the national authorities responsible for budget policies, the interaction between supranational monetary policy and **national budgetary policies** requires actions to stop differences in behaviour between *national poli-*

cies in a timely and effective manner. To ensure the success of such action and to set in motion a virtuous cycle, national policies must deviate as little as possible from the stable path.

Obviously, it is not easy to correct trends that strongly contradict basic economic variables, as these trends hide structural problems that are neither quickly nor easily solved.

There is a problem with the **potentially conflicting** nature of the interaction between **monetary policy** ("dominated" by monetary stability requirements, taken as the constitutional foundation of the EMU) and **economic policies** based on development and growth needs, and influenced by short to medium-term variables that will affect the economic context in which budgetary policy operates.

The Maastricht model of *fiscal policy coordination* requires Member States to implement their economic policies in order to contribute to the achievement of the Union's objectives. Furthermore, Member States must consider their economic policies as a *question of common interest* and coordinate them within the European Council.

The procedure is important because it does not take on the entire **stabilisation policy** at the European level. Instead, it leaves the main responsibility for ensuring economic policy coordination at the national level. This coordination is an attempt to avoid the risk of *asynchronism* in stabilisation policies, whereby while one country implements an expansionary policy while another applies a different policy. The target is to guide national economic policies towards convergent objectives through multilateral supervision.

Budgetary Coordination Procedure

The EU and the EMU also differ significantly in fiscal policy. Thus, while all EU Member States are interested in *"soft coordination"* based on the legal concept of *"matters of common concern"* (Article 121 (1) TFEU), stricter requirements and additional governance rules apply to EMU Member States.

Procedural issues affect the substantive and political aspects (the Commission maintains a technical approach, the Council a political one) such as governance of the Economic Monetary Union.

The procedural framework has **constitutional implications**: in fact, the very design of fiscal consolidation rules (an extremely complex design developed with various instruments, from the *Stability and Growth Pact* to the *Fiscal Compact*) is relatively new compared to constitutional law traditions, all fuelled by the historical "federalist" scheme. According to the latter, any separation between an economic and a monetary union is illogical.

The current design of the EMU's institutional framework seeks to overcome this conceptual difficulty.

> *"In this context, the underlying logic of reinforcing budgetary supervision by developing a fiscal consolidation legal framework is that it will serve to fill the design gap of the* EMU*, thus guaranteeing that the Union would be in a position to back up its currency* [...]. *Fiscal constraints would then, the theory goes, minimise 'moral hazard', which arises when governments may feel protected by the rest of the Union and incur higher debts than they otherwise would"* [V.R. ALMENDRAL, in T. BEUKERS *et al.* (2017)].

Here we have an important deviation from the theoretical model of fiscal federalism which requires a supranational transfer of stabilisation policy.

The distinctive feature of the current legal framework is the establishment of a *budgetary coordination procedure*.

The need for some kind of model framing budgetary coordination in a monetary union is obvious. Another issue is whether the current model is functional.

Responsibility for stabilisation policy is left to the Member States, even though coordination and supervision must be guaranteed at supranational level. In this scenario, Member States' **sovereignty** is from a legal point of view substantially **limited**.

Future institutional evolution will tell whether this delicate balance will remain in the form of "discipline" or if it will evolve into a new framework.

The Fear of Debt

The current state of interaction between monetary and economic policies can be summed up as follows: on the one hand, one of the most important implications of the transition to a *common monetary policy* is that it provides a solution to the problem that has disturbed international trade and monetary relations for decades. It makes it possible to reconcile *freedom of trade*, *full mobility* of *capital*, and *exchange rate stability*. On the other hand, EMU Member States can only maintain efficient resource allocation and economic coexistence by *unifying economic policy*.

The solution based on a strong central bank, free from political constraints and with margins of discretion, is *not* in itself *definitive*.

Monetary union led to the expectation of macroeconomic policy in which stability did not require an absolute *Bundesbank* model that only suited Germany.

There was, rather, a major aspiration: that without resorting to competitive devaluation, euro membership would imply some degree of **shared control** over the use of **fiscal transfers**.

The premises of the consequences of undisciplined fiscal policy are clearly stated:

> *"When joining a monetary union a country gives up one of its two macroeconomic instruments – monetary policy – but retains full control of the other – fiscal policy. Without national monetary policy, fiscal policy is the only instrument remaining with which to deal with asymmetric shocks when they arise.* [...]
> *In much the same way as unrestrained monetary policy eventually delivers inflation, undisciplined fiscal policy results in high public indebtedness"* [R. BALDWIN, C. WYPLOSZ (2019)].

The growth of **debt** can destabilize a country and this phenomenon can be contagious within the Eurozone.

In principle, it is in the interest of each country to resist the distortion of the deficit and there is no need for collective measures unless **spillovers** can be identified.

In fact, the **fear of debt** is based on the expectation of undermining the Eurozone's **credibility**.

The EMU legal system identifies the ECB's independence from government as the appropriate response to governments that ask the central bank to finance their deficits and to a country's propensity for heavy public debt as a sign of fiscal indiscipline that could trouble the credibility of the Eurozone;

> *"In the monetary union, a country's debt in euro is as if it were in a foreign currency, and therefore subject to sudden desertion by investors, as happens in emerging countries that typically have debt in a foreign currency"* [L. RECHLIN, in G. AMATO *et al.* (2018)].

In real federal states, sub-federal governments are usually limited in their ability to manage deficits and thus to use fiscal policy as a macroeconomic instrument.

Consistent with the non-federal architecture, the **mutualisation of debt** in the euro area is seen as a way to introduce ‘fiscal federalism’ and is therefore opposed by Germany, the Netherlands and the other small countries forming an informal alliance, the so-called “Hanseatic League”. Consequently, the legal and financial framework for common debt issuance with a common guarantee on the basis of a common **budgetary policy** was totally absent from EU policy until a **substantial common debt capacity** appeared to be the only way to counter negative macroeconomic shocks, due to the **pandemic crisis**.

The EU’s New Common Debt: the *“Recovery (Next Generation) Fund”*

In this context, the *impact of the pandemic*, the worst global economic crisis since the second World War, has represented the turning point for the issuance of **EU sovereign bonds**.

As a response to the crisis, the EU Council **Report** (9 April 2020) gave the mandate to the Commission to propose the establishment of a common fund (“*Recovery Fund*”) for the European Union with the possibility of long-term debt focused on economic recovery without mutualising debt obligations (or, rather, creating a common debt but only within this fund). This fund would be

> *“temporary, targeted and commensurate with the extraordinary costs of the current crisis and help spread them over time through appropriate financing”* [Council of the EU, *Report on the comprehensive economic policy response to the COVID-19 pandemic* (sec.19) 9 April 2020].

Working with **common debt instruments** appears to be a lesson from the previous Eurozone debt crisis, which showed that Eurozone countries should pursue a more unified economic response to the new (symmetric) crisis.

The EU pattern of an *“exceptional and temporary”* fund, issuing bonds with the EU guarantee, required the Commission to manage it through a larger budget under the *Multiannual Financial Framework* (MFF) 2021-2027.

The EU Communication, adopted on 27 May 2020 under the title *Europe's moment: Repair and Prepare for the Next Generation,* was addressed to the EU Council with the proposal aimed at setting up a *"new recovery instrument, called* ***Next Generation European Union*** *within a revamped long-term EU budget"* (NGEU) doubling its own resource ceiling to 2% of EU gross national income. This will allow the Commission to use its very strong credit rating to borrow €750 billion on the financial markets that will transform the EU into a **major player** on **bond markets**.

The EU Council Special Meeting (on 17-21 July 2020) approved the package, thus authorising the Commission *"to borrow funds on behalf of the Union on the capital markets"*.

On 17 September 2020, the Commission then issued the "*Guidance to Member States Recovery and Resilience Plans*" (SWD (2020) 205 final, 17.9.2020) for plans to be adopted by the Member States to receive this nascent financial instrument.

The new framework, built on a joint Franco-German vision, will **for the first time in history** take the model of a **fiscal power**, endowed with the capacity to raise its **own resources** (based on a plastic tax, carbon border fees and possibly a new digital tax) and **expenditure power** that channels the funds raised (to be repaid through future EU budgets, not before 2028 and not after 2058) through EU programmes.

> *"The repayment shall be scheduled, in accordance with the principle of sound financial management, so as to ensure the steady and predictable reduction in liabilities until 31 December 2058"* [**EU COUNCIL**, I, A 7].

The management of the **NGEU Funds** will entail significant **constitutional** development through the new mission of the EU *Budgetary Authority* and a *monitoring procedure.*

As regards the former, the EU Council stated that

> *"the NGEU amounts channelled through the budget for expenditure shall constitute external assigned revenues. The Budgetary Authority shall exercise political control, to be defined in agreement between the European Parliament, the Council and the Commission"* [A 11].

As regards the monitoring procedure, the single steps involve the

Commission's assessment of the national *"recovery and resilience plans"* within two months of their submission and the approval of the plans by the Council *"by qualified majority on a Commission proposal, through an implementing act which the Council shall endeavour to adopt within 4 weeks of the proposal"*.

Once the plans have been approved, the payment requests will be subject to the satisfactory achievement of the relevant milestones and targets.

Surveillance will be pursued by the Commission requiring the opinion of the *Economic and Financial Committee* of the *European Parliament*.

There remains a role for the EU Council at the request of one or more Member States: the red flag is considered to be "exceptionally" recurrent.

> *"If, exceptionally, one or more Member States consider that there are serious deviations from the satisfactory fulfilment of the relevant milestones and targets, they may request the President of the European Council to refer the matter to the next European Council.*
> [In the event, no] *approval of payments will be taken until the next European Council has exhaustively discussed the matter"* [I, A 19].

EU-UK Fiscal Capacity in the Pandemic Crisis

The EMU's *"innovative financial instruments"* are instead framed within the existing procedures. In particular, the *European Stability Mechanism* (ESM) has an autonomous lending capacity. It was created (*supra* Ch. 7) as the euro area bailout instrument to address the 2010-2012 sovereign debt crisis; the granting of loans is associated with strong conditions in terms of budgetary discipline on the borrowers' side to avoid creating negative incentives. To cope with the economic shock of the pandemic, however, credit lines, exclusively dedicated to direct or indirect healthcare spending, will be released without invasive conditions.

The ESM is in itself an instrument to provide **emergency credit lines**. This says a lot about the current institutional architecture of the EMU: to function properly it requires an *existential threat*, such as an emergency or a deep recession.

It is only in these circumstances that the currency system is able to transfer resources within the Eurozone, fulfilling a *quasi-fiscal capacity* and keeping national public debt at a manageable level.

In the mentioned context, the ECB remains the most credible advocate of monetary union. The ESM may have an ancillary function in fostering an indirect role for the ECB as *lender of last resort,* insofar as the issuance of a credit line to a Member State allows the ECB to purchase bonds from that Member State in unlimited quantities (the *"Enhanced Conditions Credit Line"*).

In this way, a *vulnerable currency union* manages to survive *de facto* without taking an important step towards federalism but without risking another Eurozone sovereign debt crisis.

On the other hand, an autonomous sovereign institution like the Bank of England – unlike the ECB – can directly finance *government spending*, allowing the Treasury to bypass the government bond market. This is not – strictly – government monetary financing, but rather a *temporary source of short-term liquidity* to support the orderly functioning of the market.

The UK government will continue to use the debt market through the operations managed by the *Debt Management Office* as the main source of funding, but has an additional instrument for emergency times, through the Bank of England's credit line (the *Ways and Means*, W&M overdraft). W&M operates currently, in a period marked by the pandemic crisis, as it operated during the financial crisis in the first decade of the century.

Monetary financing by the ECB is not allowed – in any form – by the Treaties (Article 123 TFEU) which prohibit national central banks from granting overdraft or other credit facilities to national governments or other public authorities, thus excluding the possibility of direct monetary financing of deficits.

However, from a material point of view, there is a limited difference between the W&M overdraft facility and *Quantitative Easing* (QE), e.g. the *asset purchase program* (including corporate bonds) pursued by the ECB.

Both measures are considered temporary, but QE has been rather permanent in recent years. Although technically very different, the unprecedented *Pandemic Emergency Purchase Programme* (PEPP) is broadly aligned with the W&M facility which entails for the ECB the potential unlimited obligation to intervene:

> *"In essence the ECB is committed to acting as if it were the national central bank of every member. Since it issues the world's second-most accepted reserve currency, it has the capacity to do so"* [M. WOLF, *Why the ECB can save the eurozone*, in *Financial Times*, 21 April 2020].

Strategically however, QE is not an exceptional instrument as it does not limit a further increase in public debt. Monetary financing in the EMU institutional system remains politically divisive and at odds with the entrenched paradigm of institutional euro policy, a fiscally conservative approach that has dominated the twenty and more years of euro construction.

The *Escape Clause* from the Stability and Growth Pact

The need for fiscal discipline in the EMU was recognized from the outset, leading directly to the abovementioned *Stability and Growth Pact* (SGP). The Pact seemed to suffer from a fundamental contradiction: it seeks to impose discipline on national governments, but Member States retain sovereignty in the matter.

This is why some proposals aim to establish an 'economic government for Europe', including a *European Finance Minister*. The idea is that decentralized fiscal policies should be subject to objectives of overall coherence.

Recognizing that it was too rigid to be enforceable, governments and the Commission prepared to reformulate the Pact. In a new version (adopted in 2005) the Pact was *strengthened* in a way that led to an invasion of national budgetary sovereignty.

The great financial crisis ruled out strict application of the SGP and almost all countries were technically in excessive debt.

This led to another re-engineering of the SGP, followed by a new Treaty, the *Treaty on Stability, Coordination and Governance* (*TSCG*, also called the *Fiscal Compact*), adopted in 2012. It requires each country to adopt a fiscal rule at the highest level of legislation, in order to raise budgetary discipline to a national constitutional obligation.

The first intention was to adopt the TSCG (or the "*Fiscal Compact*") within the EU legal order. After the UK's rejection, it was agreed that the new Treaty would be a purely **intergovernmental instrument** adopted outside the EU framework, albeit with institutional ties to it.

The SGP – as permanent discipline – applies to all EU Member States, but only Eurozone countries are subject to corrective action on budgetary discipline.

A new version of the SGP was enacted in 2013 and on its basis each Member State defines its own *medium-term objective*, the budget balance that it commits to achieve within a 3-year period. It must be compatible with *minimum benchmarks* estimated by the European Commission. The benchmarks recognize the starting point for each country (budget balance, debt, growth) and are updated every three years.

The SGP reform also introduced the *European semester.* The semester starts in January with the publication of the SGP forecasts for the coming years, a way to harmonize expectations and limit overly optimistic national forecasts leading to unrealistic budget forecasts. Then, in early spring, each EU government presents its *Stability and Convergence Programme*. Along with other policy objectives, the programme includes *'medium-term budgetary strategies'*, essentially a declaration of intent covering the next three years.

If a Member State adopts a budget that does not meet the requirements established by the Council, the Member considered at risk of imbalances is subject to an *in-depth review*. If these imbalances are confirmed, the Member State becomes part of the *excessive imbalance procedure*:

> *"warnings and recommendations follow in quick succession. The ultimate sanction is a fine of 0.2 per cent of the country's GDP, which takes the form of an interest-bearing deposit; these resources are frozen until the procedure is lifted."* [...]*"the decision is adopted by the Council* [...] *through a procedure called reversed qualified majority voting* [...]. *This means that the Commission's proposal is adopted unless a majority of votes, weighted by country size, decides against it. The intention is to make Commission proposals more likely to be adopted. The preventive arm applies to all EU countries but fines can be imposed only on Eurozone member countries"* [R. BALDWIN, C. WYPLOSZ (2019)].

Flexibility margins are however provided by the SGP. In particular, a *"general escape clause"* in the EU fiscal framework allows *"the flexibility necessary to national budget to support the economy"*. The conditions for the "escape clause" were deemed to have been met, in order to cope with the *"severe economic downturn in the eu-*

ro area or the Union as a whole" caused by the *"pandemic impact"*.

The Escape Clause was adopted by the **EU Council Report** on the basis of the previous communication from the Commission *on the activation of the general escape clause of the Stability and Growth Pact* [**EU Communication**, 20 March 2020].

The **escape clause** is laid down in Regulations (EC) 1466/97 and 1467/97 to facilitate the coordination of budgetary policies in times of severe economic downturn. In such a case, the Council may decide, on the recommendation of the Commission, to adopt a *revised fiscal trajectory*.

The conditions for assessing the clause were considered fulfilled by the **EU Communication**:

> *"Specifically, as the crisis is an event that is outside the control of governments with a major impact on public finances"* [it allows]*"for a coordinated and orderly temporary deviation from the normal requirements for all Member States in a situation of generalised crisis caused by a severe economic downturn of the euro area or the EU as a whole"*.

This is a measure that – albeit extraordinary – does not suspend SGP procedures, but allows *policy coordination* to depart from the budgetary requirements that would normally apply. However, this derogation - intended to be valid until 2022 – will be the premise for the reform of measures widely perceived as overly complex and unable to cope with a symmetrical economic crisis:

> ***"Member States should continue to provide targeted and temporary fiscal support in 2021 in a context where the General Escape Clause is activated, while safeguarding fiscal sustainability in the medium term.*** *They should gradually shift from a protective emergency response to measures that facilitate a reallocation of resources, and support the recovery. When economic conditions allow, fiscal policies should aim at restoring prudent medium term fiscal positions and ensuring debt sustainability, while enhancing investment.*
>
> *"Replenishing fiscal buffers over time will be important to be prepared for future crises. The activation of the General Escape Clause does not suspend the procedures of the Stability and Growth Pact"* (original font in bold) [COM (2020) 575 final, 17.9.2020].

Against this background, the *NGEU Recovery Plans*, to be presented by the Member States by 30 April 2021, will represent – de facto – an instrument of **coordination** of monetary and fiscal policy

> *"to contribute to effectively address challenges identified in the relevant country "from" specific recommendations addressed to the Member State concerned or in other relevant documents officially adopted by the Commission in the European Semester"* (SWD (2020) 205 final, 17.9.2020 n.7)

"L'Avenir: Franco-Allemande"

Even in light of the post-Brexit *British approach*, the EU-27 Member States will still need to provide a more structural solution to fiscal discipline, which is still a work in progress.

The prospects are, as always in Europe, linked to the convergence process between France and Germany.

The *"avenir"* as a *"perspective franco-allemande"* is the title of a collection of essays. The preface by Bruno Le Maire, *Ministre de l'Economie et des Finances*, recalls the points where convergence has already been achieved, even though the implementation process will take a few years. As for budgetary policy, the objective is a budget for the Eurozone:

> *"notre union monétaire ne peut être solide que si notre union économique est réelle. Le budget aura vocation è favoriser la convergence économique dans la zone euro, en finançant de projet commun et en protégeant les pays le plus faibles en cas de chocs économiques"* [B. LE MAIRE, in G. KALFLECHE *et al.* (2018)].

Once again, this confirms the trend towards a clear distinction between the EU and EMU legal orders: the issue of *economic convergence* remains an exclusive Eurozone theme.

In fact, the point made in the above quotation is not, for the time being, fully shared by the *"partenaire allemand"*:

> *"mais sans solidarité et sans convergence économique au niveau de la zone, une union économique et monétaire est un projet inabouti"* [*Ibid*].

The challenges for the future can perhaps find a window of opportunity in the **institutional changes** that will derive from the weakening of the "outs" due to the exit of the most important country in that area:

> *"Because formal institutional changes already must be made, proposals to overhaul the EU architecture of executive power might conceivably emerge as elements of a package deal that can win the endorsement of the member states committed to the European cause"* [F. FABBRINI, in T. GINSBURG, M.D. ROSEN, G. VANBERG (2019)].

At the same time, the collective effort of the two major economies in setting up the €750 billion Recovery Fund may prove decisive in promoting fiscal coordination. The implications here may be extremely wide-ranging, including the creation of the *euro sovereign fixed-income market* and increasing the top-rated debt. A deeper bond market would also improve the euro's standing.

The issuance of EU **sovereign bonds** to finance the *Recovery Fund* has undoubtedly the potential to enhance

> *"the euro's role as a reserve currency by creating a new safe asset that can be used as collateral in the money market. This institutional shift may in time become even more influential than the fund itself"* [*Financial Times*, 23 July 2020].

There is no doubt that the above implications, potentially transforming the international monetary landscape, were among the founding reasons for the common vision *"de l'avenir"* that led to the establishment of a *federal deficit* as an instrument of managing macroeconomic crises. An instrument providing for *fiscal transfers* and shared fiscal mechanisms that – although justified for emergency reasons –for the first time gives meaning to the concept of **financial solidarity** in the short term. A coordinated and systemic **policy** response to external symmetric shock, targeting macroeconomic stabilization, will became in the medium-long term a powerful tool for the construction of a **fiscal union**.

EU-UK Governance: the *Partnership Council*

The governance of a partnership such as the one envisaged by the **Political Declaration** and then implemented (although it is still far from including all areas of the two economies) by the **Trade and Cooperation Agreement** that entered into force on January 1, 2021, has been entrusted to a newly devised **Partnership Council**.

The *Council* (established by the **TCA**, Part 1, Title III), composed of representatives of the Parties and co-chaired by a UK Minister and an EU Commissioner, has been called upon to supervise and facilitate the implementation and enforcement of the Agreement. It is a typical joint body and so far it can only make its decisions and recommendations by mutual agreement. However, in several cases, it has a role in proposing amendments to certain aspects of the **TCA**, subject to applicable internal requirements and procedures.

As mentioned above (*Introduction*), the **governance framework** appears to be more robust as far as the **compliance mechanism** founded by the **TCA** than in terms of the "*Institutional Provisions*" regarding obligations to be fulfilled by the Parties.

The enforcement mechanism focuses (as stated in the Commission **Explanatory Memorandum**) on *"the possibility for the Parties to take swift, autonomous and operational measures to protect their interests"*.

Specifically, reference is made to enforcement measures in the areas of a*level playing field* (i.e. *rebalancing measures, remedial measures*)

> *"as well as, more generally, in cases of serious economic, societal or environmental difficulties of a sectorial or regional nature"* [Explanatory Memorandum, p. 7].

It is a governance framework, in other words, that while encouraging cooperation, envisages on a more concrete level appropriate unilateral measures for each Party to *protect itself* against the effects on trade or investments resulting from significant divergences in the respective regulatory systems.

It is a framework designed by looking realistically at the future of the two **global economies** acting definitively as **separate markets**.

Chapter 9
GLOBAL

"The situation of Great Britain,
the character of her people and the
nature of her government,
fit her for trade and commerce [...]
The sea is our barrier, ships are our
fortresses, and the mariners, that trade
and commerce alone can furnish,
are the garrisons to defend them".
(BOLINGBROKE, Secretary of State, 1738)

Competing in Trade Policy

The above words recall the remote, historical approach of Great Britain in avoiding any entanglement on the continent, giving instead "her 'continual attention to improve her natural, that is the maritime strength'. The myth of the British separateness from Europe was born" [B. HEUSER (2019)].
As preeminent global power emerged from Napoleonic wars,

> *"Britain was carrier for the world and Lloyd's of London insured this shipping. After Waterloo, the pound sterling became the preferred currency for almost all international trade and commercial transactions"* [A. BOYD (2020)]

Free Trade Agreements (FTAs) have been at the heart of British history and the ideal of a ***blue sea power****, often used as an alternative to war.*

History is full of examples:

> *"Thus the Anglo-French commercial treaty of 1860 was seen as an alternative to war or an arms race with Napoleon III. Free Trade not*

> *military force – so the argument ran – would keep the peace in Europe"* [B. SIMMS (2016)].

Vice versa, when Britain cancelled a trade treaty with Germany thirty years later, the choice was closely linked to the rebuff of Bismarck's proposal of an alliance and the confidence that the "sea-power" influence would in itself dissuade the military force of the new German state:

> *"The German Kaiser Wilhelm II remarked bitterly that (if) we had a strong, respected enduring fleet, then this abrogation would never have happened"* [*Ibid*].

In the contemporary era of ***trade relations****, on the basis of the Treaties, the EU signed a huge number of agreements with third countries. They give rise to separate EU bilateral agreements covering trade in goods and (to a lesser extent) in services and regulating customs.*

The UK as a "third country" has now entered into the equivalent of a legal vacuum in key parts of its external trade relations, rapidly trying to fill the vacuum through the signing of FTAs.

As to the trade relationship between the EU and the UK, the ***Political Declaration*** *set out the objective of developing – between the Parties – a*

> *"wide-ranging and balanced economic partnership. This partnership will be comprehensive, encompassing a Free Trade Agreement, as well as wider sectoral cooperation where it is in the mutual interest of both Parties"* (sec. 17).

The result was achieved, as known, with the signing – at the very last minute before the expiry of the Transition Period on 31 December 2020 – of the ***Trade and Cooperation Agreement.***

The ***TCA*** *now gives rise to two* ***separate markets*** *and* ***distinct legal orders as*** *envisaged – as mentioned since the beginning – by the* ***Political Declaration.***

It seems natural to assume one ("separate markets") as the premise of the other ("distinct legal orders") and vice versa. Legal concepts are certainly relevant to explaining an economic system. At the same time, the economic system influences the structure of the institutional environment; the explanation of the context of economic and institutional structures is unified.

The ***TCA,*** *on the EU side, is the result of a negotiation process managed by adopting "a very united stance vis-à-vis a withdrawing state"*

[F. FABBRINI (2020)]; *on the UK side it will require the reconciliation of two (originally) different perspectives:*

> *"a new nationalism – 'taking back control' – together with a new internationalism – 'the UK as a global free trade champion'"* [K.A. ARMSTRONG (2017)].

In global terms, a return "to a time when the country was fully sovereign and simultaneously able to play a global role" would imply a debate on the "Anglo sphere as a geopolitical alternative to the European Union" [E. CAMPANELLA, M. DASSÙ, 2019].

Against this background, negotiating the "envisaged new partnership" has required a shared vision of the future relationship focusing on "free trade" and ensuring access to "goods" and (in a limited way) to "services".

The process will not involve alignment: it will likely be the starting point for the creation of ***new concepts*** *and* ***a new trade framework****, which could ultimately prove to be of mutual benefit, in a context of competition between models of* ***economic competitiveness****.*

Customs Union and Trade Policy

The first political act issued by the EU institutions after exit day was the European Commission's **Recommendation for a Council Decision** (on 3 February 2020) *"authorising the opening of negotiations for a new partnership with the United Kingdom of Great Britain and Northern Ireland"*. The envisaged "*new partnership*" would require – according to the Commission Recommendation –

> *"general arrangements (including provisions on basic values and principles and on governance); economic arrangements (including provisions on trade and level playing field guarantees)"* (sec. 3).

The Commission Recommendation was then followed by the European Council decisions on the **Directives for negotiation** (on 25 February 2020) which pursued the same path.

A "Free Trade Area" – as envisaged for the "new partnership" –

is exactly the core of the inception of the Treaty of Rome in 1957.

The intention of the Treaty of Rome was to create a unified economic area within which all companies and consumers would have equal opportunities to buy or sell goods and services.

The most obvious requirement was to remove "trade" barriers, i.e. all tariffs and quantitative restrictions among Member States. Even in contemporary times – as in the days of "sea power" – governments can be committed to developing tariff and quota-like barriers against foreign goods and services (as exemplified by recent US trade policy).

On the other hand, trade can never be truly free among nations unless they harmonize their **trade policy** towards non-members. If members had different tariffs towards a third country, there would be an incentive to circumvent them.

The Treaties avoid this risk by requiring Member States to adopt a *'common commercial policy',* i.e. identical restrictions on imports from **non-members**. With these restrictions, every Member State can be sure that every product physically located within the EU has been paid for with the common tariff and has met common requirements, for example, on health and safety standards.

The **customs union** allows goods to circulate within the EU legal order: Member States also apply the same import duties to goods arriving from the rest of the world. These agreed duties are known as the *Common External Tariffs*, or *Common Customs Tariffs*. Once the tariff is paid, upon entry into a Member State, the goods can move freely within the common market.

Even a *customs union* is not sufficient to create a *unified economic area*. Trade liberalization can be offset by public and private measures operating within its borders.

The Treaties therefore require that competition in the area should not be distorted: this includes – as we have already seen – *prohibitions on trade-distorting subsidies* for national producers, the creation of a common *competition policy* and the harmonisation of national laws affecting the *functioning of the internal market*. To reduce the deviation from a unified economic area, the EU harmonizes product standards and regulations:

> *"the EU's power on trade policy was basically limited to tariffs, [as] tariffs were by far the most important aspect of trade policy [...] [As] the nature of international commerce grew more complex, the range of important trade barriers broadened.*

As the logic of a unified external trade policy was stronger than ever, this trend created a need to expand the competence of the EU beyond tariffs. This was done in a series of small and practical steps […] *which extended the Common Commercial Policy to explicitly include trade in services, foreign direct investment and some aspects of intellectual property rights (copyrights, patents, etc.)"* [R. BALDWIN, C. WYPLOSZ (2019)].

All this led to the EU becoming a **real power** in global trade,

"as negotiator of trade agreements and as an originator and exporter of market regulations, the latter function is particularly interesting. The very construction of the single market has required the formulation and imposition of regulations governing the production and circulation of commodities within the EU" [A. CALLINICOS, in E. NANOPOULOS, F. VERGIS (2019)].

The EU as a "Global Regulatory Power"

The emergence of the European Union as a **global rule-maker** created a borderless pan-European market for goods that triggered a process of *regulatory convergence* among non-EU countries, creating powerful incentives for their adoption.

The Union accounts for approximately a **third** of world trade.

Four of the remaining 27 EU Member States are ranked among the top ten trading nations in the world (Germany, France, Italy, and the Netherlands). The EU is also a leader in the world trading system as a key player in the *World Trade Organization* (WTO) and in forging WTO agreements.

As said, *trade policy* is an ***exclusive competence*** of the EU:

"The common commercial policy (trade policy) is one of the Union's longest-standing exclusive competences. It has been exclusive since the establishment of the customs union […] *This means that as an EU Member State the UK has not had (and could not have had as a matter of EU law) a national trade policy"* [M. CREMONA, in M. DOUGAN (2017)].

Thus, the EU has the exclusive power to determine trade policy with "third countries". This is the core of the common commercial policy. The rationale of not allowing individual Member States to legislate on trade matters or to conclude **international trade** agreements is clear: if each member were allowed to conclude bilateral agreements on its own, the single market would be undermined by **third countries** exploiting the differences between the **external trade policies of EU members**.

Trade agreements with third parties and international agreements provide European companies with a network of market access rights for non-EU-countries: the Commission's larger negotiating power allows Member States "*to achieve ends that might not be possible for individual states*" [J. MORPHET (2017)].

Indeed, trade policy has also been one of the EU's most effective **foreign policy instruments**. Since the Lisbon Treaty, the dividing lines between foreign policy and trade policy have become ever more blurred. The Lisbon Treaty established a *hierarchy of principles* to be applied to trade policy (as well as to all other aspects of foreign policy). For example, Article 3(5) TEU reiterates that:

> *"In its relations with the wider world, the Union shall uphold and promote its values and interests and contribute to the protection of its citizens. It shall contribute to peace, security, the sustainable development of the Earth, solidarity and mutual respect among peoples, free and fair trade".*

The recent literature, based on the assumptions of the EU's **global regulatory power** and influence, has theorized a *"Brussels Effect"*. The concept refers to the fact that:

> *"the EU has the ability to promulgate regulations that shape the global business environment, leading to a notable "Europeanization" of many important aspects of global commerce. Different from many other forms of global influence, the EU does not need to impose its standards coercively on anyone – market forces alone are often sufficient to convert the EU standard into the global standard as companies voluntarily extend the EU rule to govern their worldwide operations"* [A. BRADFORD (2020)].

On the basis of these factual assumptions, the emergence of **unilateral regulatory globalization** can be expected.

> *"The Brussels Effect leads to "unilateral regulatory globalization", where regulations originating from a single jurisdiction penetrate many aspects of economy life across the global marketplace"* [*Ibid*].

These concepts have been relevant for the Trade Deal between the EU and the UK, in particular with regard to goods. The assumption is that access to an EU-wide market will still require the adoption of *EU standards,* such as "**rules of origin**", i.e. control over the regulatory conditions (social, environmental, health) necessary for access to the large EU consumer market. The issue is now regulated by the **TCA** (Part 2, Title I, Chapters 2 and 3) ensuring – on the basis of appropriate rules of origin – that only "*originating*" goods are able to benefit from the liberalized access arrangement agreed in the **TCA**, reflecting the requirements of UK and EU industry. This reduces the prospect of UK *regulatory freedom* for *trade* in goods: rules of origins and technical norms (conformity assessment, standardisation, accreditation, etc.) are much **stricter than the equivalence criteria** used in the financial services sector.

The point is clearly stated by the EU Commission:

> *"All imports from the United Kingdom will have to satisfy Union rules and regulations (e.g. technical rules and product standards, sanitary or phytosanitary rules, regulations on food and safety, health and safety standards, environmental protection, consumer protection)"* [**Explanatory Memorandum**, 25.12.2020].

The role of the EU as "global regulator" is in fact the effect of the behaviour of market players complying independently with EU regulatory policy.

A point highlighted in the literature on the external scope of EU regulatory standards:

> *"Larger firms with significant cross-border activities may consider it to be in their interest to continue to comply with EU rules. As the concept of the "Brussels Effect" highlights, this continued compliance with Single Market rules may extend beyond the Single Market activities of non-EU firms to include their UK operations insofar as compliance with EU norms meets and exceeds less stringent UK regulatory demands"* [K.A. ARMSTRONG, in S. BULMER, L. QUAGLIA (2018)].

The prospect is one of **regulatory competition** between policy rule-makers.

> *"Both the UK and the EU will face competitive influences at a global level. Indeed, the issue for the UK and the EU may be how best to seek to influence the global regulatory environment in order to manage regulatory competition"* [*Ibid*].

In **institutional** terms, *trade policy* gives rise to a "**centralized administration**".

The allocation of responsibilities involves all major EU institutions.

The *European Commission* is responsible for negotiating trade issues with third countries on behalf of Member States (Article 3(1) TFEU). The Commission takes the lead on trade policy in the sense that, for example, it has the right of initiative on trade agreements and is responsible for implementing and monitoring compliance with existing agreements and WTO rules.

In practice, this means that the *EU Trade Commissioner* is responsible for trade negotiations. These negotiations are conducted in accordance with specific mandates defined by the EU Council and the European Parliament (called *Directives for negotiation*).

As regards **procedure**, decisions are taken according to the "ordinary legislative procedure" which provides for majority voting in the Council and Parliament. The Council must adopt the agreements negotiated by the Commission after Parliament's approval. The European Parliament is now co-legislator with the Council on all basic EU trade legislation. In addition, the Commission is required to keep Parliament regularly informed about ongoing negotiations.

"Set in a silver sea"

"This precious stone set in the silver sea" [*Richard II, Act II, Scene I*] recalls the UK's enduring ability to trade and inspires suggestions for the new "free trade area" with the EU.

In political and international terms, historians note that:

> *"Britain… is primarily a continental story, that her destiny was mainly determined by relations with the rest of Europe rather than with the wider world"* [B. SIMMS (2016)].

In economic terms, the prevalence of relations with the rest of

Europe is well known: the EU remains the UK's most important trading partner.

> *"Both the UK and EU Member States benefit from our close trading relationship. The EU is the UK's largest export market and the UK is the largest goods export market for the EU27 taken as a whole".* [H.M. UK Gov. (2017)].

According to IMF 2019 figures, the UK sends 47% of its exports to the rest of the EU compared to 15% to the US (*Financial Times*, 27 December 2020).

On the other hand, in the public opinion debate Britain is seen as a beacon of free trade and a destination for global companies: not so much (as in the past) a superpower, but still *"a global power"*.

Being "global" would therefore mean expanding the network of *free trade* and *economic liberalism,* even though, in fact, the new FTAs signed by the UK (as demonstrated by the trade agreements signed by the UK with Canada, Japan and other countries during the Transition period) are *"continuity agreements"* that largely replicate the corresponding existing agreements with the EU-third countries.

On the other hand, bilateral trade agreements signed by the EU provide EU companies with access on more favourable conditions than those guaranteed by WTO membership. In trade terms, the advantage of the internal market is the size of the market itself. The "global" effect is implicit in the fact that non-EU-countries negotiate access for their companies to around 450 million EU customers.

The Building of the *EU-UK Trade and Cooperation Agreement*

At the beginning, the UK's official position was presented in the following terms, devising a market in Europe for a 27 plus-one relationship.

> *"It is in the interests of the EU and all parts of the UK for the deeply integrated trade and economic relationship between the UK and EU to be maintained after our exit from the EU. Our new relationship should aim for the freest possible trade in goods and services between the UK and the EU. It should give UK companies the maximum freedom to trade with and operate within European markets and let Euro-*

> *pean businesses do the same in the UK. This should include a new customs agreement with the EU, which will help to support our aim of trade with the EU that is as frictionless as possible"* [White Paper (2017)].

The Parties' official positions were then expressed in the **Political Declaration** in a formulation consistent with each party's (different) policies. Still, the document reaffirms "*the integrity of the Single Market and the Customs Union and the indivisibility of the four freedoms"* on the one hand and, on the other, the UK's intention to pursue "*its independent trade policy and the ending of free movement of people between the Union and the United Kingdom"* (sec. 4).

The framework of the new trade relationship with the EU was again outlined by the UK in the document submitted to Parliament for the introduction of the **European Union (Withdrawal Agreement) Bill** (later EUWA 2020). Accordingly:

> *"Within this free trade area there will be no tariffs and no fees, charges or quantitative restrictions across all sectors, and no need for checks on rules of origin".*

In fact, only complete and perfect *regulatory alignment* would enable the exclusion of controls on ***rules of origin*** that could favour a third country over a similar set of EU rules. The point is essential because

> *"the core itself of the common market and in the last instance the reason to need European integration is to set a common regulatory framework so as to prevent destructive races to the bottom"* [K. O'Rourke (2018)].

Compared with this background, the terms of the *future relationship*, despite the stated intentions, remained rather vague:

> *"On regulation, we will agree common principles on compliance processes, explore cooperation with EU agencies* [...] *and consider aligning with specific EU rules where that could help to deliver our objectives"* [**White Paper** *(November 2018)*].

Alignment would thus be conditioned by *"our objectives"*.

It is correct, on these premises, to state, as officially recognized in the same document that:

> *"No other advanced economy has this arrangement with the EU"*: in fact: *"the exact design of this regulatory and customs cooperation could lead to a spectrum of different outcomes for administrative processes, checks and controls"* [*Ibid*].

Verbal formulas are likely to hide serious conflicts of opinion. The UK Attorney General's **Legal Position** on the draft of the **Withdrawal Agreement** made it clear that, while the single customs territory is the one

> *"under which the UK aligns itself with the Union's external tariffs and there can be no tariffs or quantitative restrictions on imports and exports between the UK and the EU"* the distinct legal orders *"create new concepts that are to be interpreted in accordance with normal principles of international law"* (sec. 17).

The "principles of international law" will actually be the basis for the creation of **new concepts**. These principles will be necessary in view of the UK's "unprecedented" vision of a "fair trade" policy:

> *"We do not seek to adopt a model already enjoyed by other countries. The UK already has zero tariffs on goods and a common regulatory framework with the EU Single Market. This position is unprecedented in previous trade negotiations. Unlike other trade negotiations, this is not about bringing two divergent systems together. It is about finding the best way for the benefit of the common system and framework, that currently enable UK and EU businesses to trade with and operate in each other's markets"* [**White Paper** (2017)].

Along the same lines, on the basis of this statement of principle the subsequent **White Paper 2018** (*July 2018*) introduced a proposal for the creation of *"a free trade area for goods"*, in line with the objective of achieving an independent trade policy. The latter was rejected by the EU on the assumption that it would be equivalent to "cherry-picking".

For its part, the **Withdrawal Agreement** (Article 4), which reflected the *status quo* of the common understanding between the Parties, vaguely required the UK to harmonize its commercial policy with the EU's common commercial policy to the extent necessary for the *functioning* of the single customs territory.

Level Playing Field and Right to Regulate

In terms of definition, an FTA is a preferential trade agreement organized with a single country or a group of nations and typically includes goods and services, but not financial services.

> *"The core of a free trade agreement is the abolition of tariffs and quotas on goods. There will normally be provisions dealing with technical barriers to trade* [...] *More ambitious trade agreements aim for liberalisation in areas such as services and investment"* [P. CRAIG, in M. DOUGAN (2017)].

In fact, in a free trade area (such as the *North American Free Trade Area* (NAFTA), between Canada, the United States and Mexico, or ASEAN between South East Asian States) member states agree not to impose customs duties on products originating in other member states but are free to pursue their own trade policies with third countries. Usually an FTA – like the recent EU/*Canada Comprehensive Economic and Trade Agreement* (CETA) – is a *mixed* agreement (e.g. it involves even competence of the member states) and therefore requires ratification by states, a process that for the CETA, signed in 2016, has not yet been completed.

The CETA model was clearly envisaged by the **UK's approach to negotiations**, although trade volumes with the EU are not comparable.

The approach adopted by the UK in the mentioned position paper on this issue was essentially aimed at supporting the idea of a facilitated customs arrangement that would eliminate the need for checks and controls on goods, provided the *"relevant rules of origins"* are respected:

> *"The Agreement should provide liberalised market access for trade goods. The provisions on market access should be comprehensive and ensure there are no tariffs, fees, charges and quantitative restrictions on trade* [...] *where goods meet the relevant rules of origin"* [UK's Approach to Negotiations (2020) Part 1, sec. 3].

It seems to reflect a shift in thinking, from *"no need for checks on rules of origin"* to the necessity that *"goods meet the relevant rules"*.

From this point of view, the **UK's position** implies a **common**

rulebook to ensure that goods in circulation in the respective markets meet the necessary regulatory requirements to guarantee that only these goods *"are able to benefit from the liberalized market access arrangements"* (Part 1, sec. 5). On the other hand, arrangements should promote trade by *"preserving each party's right to regulate, as is standard in free trade agreements"* (sec. 10).

The default of a "**right to regulate**", i.e. the complete alignment of the third party with EU rules is what characterized agreements such as the one between the EU and EFTA – the *European Free Trade Association* (Norway, Lichtenstein, and Iceland) – for near-complete access to the single market (*European Economic Area* – EEA).

The EEA agreement allows EFTA states

> *"to participate in a large part of the EU's internal market and to largely enjoy the four freedoms, without being committed to other EU policies, such as agriculture, fisheries, judicial affairs, foreign policy, etc. These countries have to follow the evolution of the EU legislation concerning the internal market as well as its evolution, without having the right to really influence its content much"* [J.-C. PIRIS, in P.J. BIRKINSHAW, A. BIONDI (2016)].

In other words, they are the so-called "**rule takers**", an option – quite obviously – not acceptable by the UK.

The Parties' Negotiating Documents

In their normative drafts (i.e. the **EU Draft**, published on 18 March 2020 and the **UK Draft**, released on 19 May 2020) the Parties seemed to foresee a sort of *middle ground* between the two extremes of the spectrum.

The middle ground would exclude both *complete autonomy* in the level playing field (LPF) regulatory framework and a *rule-taker position*.

On this basis, according to the **EU Draft**, the Parties maintain their shared values in principle (e.g. by ensuring a level playing field *"necessary for trade and investment"*) and reaffirm – and even strengthen – their mutual commitment to promote shared values, in the light of *"geographic proximity and economic interdependence"*.

All this would save the *"right to regulate"* combined with the *"pre-*

cautionary principle". Consequently, on the one hand, each party has the right *"to set policies and priorities* [...] *and to adopt or modify its relevant laws and policies"*.

On the other hand, when the EU adopts a relevant *"new act or provision"*, there would be no obligation for the UK to comply with it. However, specific procedures – providing for the establishment of a joint *"Specialised Committee on the Level Playing Field and Sustainability"*– would allow the impact of the new act or provision to be verified and thus to add the new act or provision to the agreement between the parties or to *"examine all further possibilities to maintain the good functioning"* of the agreement itself.

On its side, the **UK Draft** was characterized by the prospect of a trade agreement establishing "a trade area" under the framework of the WTO agreement *"interpreted in accordance with the customary rules of public international law"*. The objective was *"to facilitate trade in goods between the Parties and to maintain liberalized trade in goods"* on the basis of elimination of *"customs duties on all goods originating in either Party"* assuming a common discipline of *"rules of origin"*.

Anti-dumping and countervailing measures were designed as *"trade remedies"* reaffirming the rights and obligations arising from the WTO agreements.

Obviously, the middle ground approach would work in a context of close cooperation, with a dispute resolution mechanism and a joint commission, all provided for in specific "Institutional Provisions" and "Dispute Settlement".

The WTO and GPA Regime

A "no bilateral trade deal" after the transition period would have paved the way for other international instruments, namely WTO rules, to regulate the EU-UK trade relationship.

The **legal issue** relating to the application of WTO rules would have concerned the rights and obligations of the UK within the WTO as a separate "party". Under the WTO multilateral agreements – and in particular the provisions of the *General Agreement on Tariffs and Trade* (GATT) and the *General Agreement on Trade in Services* (GATS) –rights and obligations are exercised and enforced by the EU *on behalf of all Member States.*

Although the point appeared controversial, it was a moot question given that the UK was in the position of a (pre-accession) WTO Member:

> *"all WTO rules that apply to WTO Members on an erga omnes parties basis also apply to the UK without any further complications"* [L. BARTELS, in R. SCHÜTZE *et al.* (2018)].

Instead, it is undisputed that the United Kingdom is not a party to the *Agreement on Government Procurement* (GPA) *per se*, as only the EU is a party to it.

The GPA – as seen (*supra* Ch. 5) – is significant as a plurilateral agreement due to the obligations of contracting entities in *public procurement procedures*.

Accession to the GPA can be based on international rules on the succession of states to the Treaties.

> *"There is a practice concerning the succession of states from unions and federations formed by them with other states. This practice is virtually uniform: in almost all cases the state resuming its autonomy succeeded to the rights and obligations in treaties entered into by that federation or union. This includes, in particular, trade agreements"* [*Ibid*].

Future Imbalance and Rebalancing

The final positions of the Parties have finally found a synthesis in the **Trade and Cooperation Agreement** ratified by the UK Parliament with the *EU* (*Future Partnership*) *Act* passed on 30 December 2020, right at the end of the Transition Period (31 December 2020) marking the day the UK - after 47 years of membership - left the Single Market and the Custom Union.

With respect to the envisaged *open fair competition,* the *non-committing statements* agreed to in the **Political Declaration** are now translated into *binding terms* (Part 2, Title XI).

On the one hand, the EU requirement of a "dynamic alignment" to the EU's level playing field provisions *"ensured through robust commitments"* was ruled out. The Agreement maintains for both the two legal orders the **right to regulate** each one's own independent system of subsidy control, as well as labour and social policy, or environment policy. Some general principles aim to ensure that regulatory changes do not alter "*open fair competition*" between the Parties.

As already said (*supra* Ch. 3), in the event that a reset of rules leads to a **regulatory imbalance in the ordinary functioning of the two competitive economies**, the Parties have agreed to a **rebalancing mechanism** that allows both Parties to take rapid action even using tariffs.

As mutually required during negotiations, a **dispute settlement mechanism** is provided through accelerated arbitration procedure and there is the possibility of compensation if the level playing field changes significantly (unnecessarily or disproportionately). In practice, the **TCA** has established a mechanism to deter the other party from **excessive regulatory divergence.**

The vague verbalism of compromised solutions required by the drafting of a common legal text is tempered – as the "file rouge" this book suggests – by **shared organizing values** that will help shape the **institutional arrangements** that will govern the relations between the Parties in the foreseeable future.

On the one hand, the legal language was decisive in allowing the political will to unlock a deal and devise a landing zone in the key area of negotiations. On the other hand, the legal clauses themselves provide a platform that allows the Parties to broadly retain the level playing field for the foreseeable future, widening in due time the Deal to other economic areas.

The outcome of the process, the signing of "a trade deal", a typical *global* issue, defines the prospective **identity** of the Parties and at the same time marks the basic elements of the new **separate markets** and **distinct legal orders**.

REFERENCES

Given the vastity of bibliography available on the themes dealt in the study, references are below reported uniquely with regard to the quotations made in the text and limited to studies published as books or as part of collectaneous works.

A) Literature

(1967) B. ABEL-SMITH, R. STEVENS, *Lawyers and the Courts*, Heinemann, London

(2019) H. ADDINK, *Good Governance: Concept and Context*, Oxford University Press

(1964) C.K. ALLEN, *Law in the Making*, 7 th ed., Oxford University Press

(2019) G. AMATO, E. MOAVERO-MILANESI, G. PASQUINO, L. REICHLIN (eds.), *The History of the European Union: Constructing Utopia*, Hart Publishing, London

(2014) A. ARLIDGE, I. JUDGE, *Magna Carta Uncovered*, Hart Publishing, Oxford and Portland, Oregon

(2017) J. ARMOUR, R. KRAAKMAN, P. DAVIES, L. ENRIQUES, H. HANSMANN, G. HERTIG, K. HOPT, H. KANDA, M. PARGENDEL, W.G. RINGE, E. ROCK,*The Anatomy of Corporate Law: A Comparative and Functional Approach*, 3rd ed. Oxford University Press, Oxford

(2017) J. ARMOUR, H. EIDENMÜLLER, *Negotiating Brexit*, Verlag C.H. Beck, München

(2017) K.A. ARMSTRONG, *Brexit Time: Leaving the EU – Why, How and When?*, Cambridge University Press

(2011) J. ATTALI, *Demain, qui gouvernera le monde?* Fayard, Paris

(2018) J. ATTALI, *Comment nous protéger des prochaines crises*,Fayard, Paris

(2019) A. BAKARDJIEVA ENGELBREKT, X. GROUSSOT (eds.), *The Future of Europe: Political and Legal Integration Beyond Brexit*, Hart Publishing, Oxford

(2019) R. BALDWIN, C. WYPLOSZ (eds.), *The Economics of European Integration*, 6th ed., McGraw – Hill Education, Berkshire

(2003) N. BAMFORTH, P. LEYLAND (eds.), *Public Law in a Multi-Layered Constitution,* Hart Publishing, Oxford and Portland, Oregon
(2006) J. BELL, C. KILPATRICK (eds.), *The Cambridge Yearbook of European Legal Studies,* Hart Publishing, Oxford and Portland, Oregon
(2016) J. BELL, M. ELLIOT, J. NE VARUHAS, P. MURRAY, *Public Law Adjudication in Common Law Systems: Process and Substance*, Hart Publishing, Oxford and Portland, Oregon
(2017) T. BEUKERS, B. de WITTE, C. KILPATRICK, *Constitutional Change through Euro-Crisis Law,* Cambridge University Press
(2015) C. J. BICKERTON, D. HODSON, U. PUETTER, *The New Intergovernmentalism: States and Supranational Actors in the Post-Maastricht Era*, Oxford University Press
(2010) T. BINGHAM, *The Rule of Law*, Penguin Books, London
(2016) P.J. BIRKINSHAW, A. BIONDI, *Britain Alone! The Implications and Consequences of United Kingdom Exit from the EU*, Kluwer Law International, Alphen aan den Rijn
(2019) J. BLACK, *Britain and Europe: A Short History*, Hurst & Company, London
(2019) V. BOGDANOR, *Beyond Brexit: Towards a British Constitution*, I.B. Tauris, London
(2019) S. BOGOJEVIĆ,X. GROUSSOT, J. HETTNE (eds.), *Discretion in EU Public Procurement Law*, Hart Publishing, Oxford
(2020) A. BOYD, *British Naval Intelligence through the Twentieth Century*, Seaforth Publishing
(2020) A. BRADFORD, *The Brussels Effect: How the European Union Rules the World*, Oxford University Press
(2016) M.K. BRUNNERMEIER, H. JAMES, J.P. LANDAU, *The Euro and the Battle of Ideas*, Princeton University Press, Princeton and Oxford
(2018) S. BULMER, L. QUAGLIA, *The Politics and Economics of Brexit*, Routledge, London
(2019) E. CAMPANELLA, M. DASSÙ, *Anglo Nostalgia: The Politics of Emotion in a Fractured West*, Oxford University Press
(2009) P. CANE, *Administrative Tribunals and Adjudication*, Hart Publishing, Portland, Oregon
(2002) P. CANE, *Responsibility in Law and Morality*, Hart Publishing, Portland, Oregon
(1941) C.T. CARR, *Concerning English Administrative Law*, Columbia University Press, New York
(2018) S. CASSESE, *A World Government?*, Global Law Press, Seville
(2004) M. CHANG, *Realigning Interests: Crisis and Credibility in European Monetary Integration*, Palgrave Macmillan
(2016) M. CHANG, *Economic and Monetary Union*, Macmillan, London
(2017) C. CLOSA (ed.), *Secession from a Member State and Withdrawal from the European Union*, Cambridge University Press

(2015) B.J. COHEN, *Currency Power: Understanding Monetary Rivalry*, Princeton University Press, Princeton and Oxford
(2012) D. CONAGHAN, *The Bank: Inside the Bank of England,* Biteback Publishing, London
(2018) A.J. CORNELL, M. GOLDONI (eds.), *National and Regional Parliaments in the EU-Legislative Procedure Post-Lisbon,* Hart Publishing, Oxford and Portland, Oregon
(2020) D. COYLE, *Markets, State, and People: Economics for Public Policy*, Princeton University Press, Princeton and Oxford
(2003) P. CRAIG, R. RAWLINGS (eds.), *Law and Administration in Europe: Essays in honour of Carol Harlow*, Oxford University Press
(2015) P. CRAIG, *UK, EU and Global Administrative Law: Foundations and Challenges*, Cambridge University Press
(1971) R. CROSS, *Precedent in English Law*, 3rd ed., Clarendon Press, Oxford
(2019) W. DARLYMPLE, *The Anarchy: The East India Company, Corporate Violence, and the Pillage of an Empire*, Bloomsbury, London
(1971) K.C. DAVIS, *Discretionary Justice: A Preliminary Inquiry*, University of Illinois Press, Urbana – Chicago – London
(1976) K.C. DAVIS, *Discretionary Justice in Europe and America*, University of Illinois Press, Urbana – Chicago – London
(2001) A.C.L. DAVIES, *Accountability: A Public Law Analysis of Government by Contract*, Oxford University Press
(2016) G. DELLA CANANEA, *Due Process of Law Beyond the State: Requirements of Administrative Procedure*, Oxford University Press
(1917) A.V. DICEY, *Lectures on the Relation Between Law and Public Opinion in England During the Nineteenth Century*, Macmillan & Co., London
(1959) A.V. DICEY, *An Introduction to the Study of the Law of the Constitution*, 10th ed., The Macmillan Press, London
(2014) D. DODD, *The Social Life of Money*, Princeton University Press, Princeton & Oxford
(2017) M. DOUGAN (ed.), *The UK after Brexit*, Intersentia, Cambridge
(1987) J. EEKELAAR, J. BELL eds., *Oxford Essays in Jurisprudence*, Clarendon Press, Oxford
(2016) L. ELLIOT, D. ATKINSON, *Europe Isn't Working*, Yale University Press, New Haven and London
(2020) F. FABBRINI, (ed.) *The Law & Politics of Brexit, II, The Withdrawal Agreement,* Oxford University Press
(2020) F. FABBRINI, *Brexit and the Future of the European Union: The Case for Constitutional Reforms,* Oxford University Press
(2017) F. FABBRINI (ed.), *The Law & Politics of Brexit*, Oxford University Press
(2008) N. FERGUSON, *The Ascent of Money: A Financial History of the World*, The Penguin Press, New York

(2006) M. FREEDLAND, J.B. AUBY (eds.), *The Public Law / Private Law Divide: Une entente assez cordiale?* Hart Publishing, Oxford and Portland, Oregon

(2019) F. FUKUYAMA, *Identity: Contemporary Identity Politics and the Struggle for Recognition*,2nd ed., Profile Books, London

(1986) D.J. GALLIGAN, *Discretionary Powers: A Legal Study of Official Discretion*, Clarendon Press, Oxford

(1996) D.J. GALLIGAN, *Due Process and Fair Procedures: A Study of Administrative Procedures*, Clarendon Press, Oxford

(2007) D.J. GALLIGAN, *Law in Modern Society*, Oxford University Press

(2014) D.J. GALLIGAN, *Constitutions and the Classics: Patterns of Constitutional Thought from Fortescue to Bentham*, Oxford University Press

(2019) L. GHIA, *International Business Law*, 2nd ed., Wolters Kluwer, Milano

(2019) T. GINSBURG, M.D. ROSEN, G. VANBERG (eds.), *Constitutions in Times of Financial Crisis (Comparative Constitutional Law and Policy)*, Cambridge University Press

(2015) M. GORDON, *Parliamentary Sovereignty in the UK Constitution: Process, Politics and Democracy*, Hart Publishing, Oxford and Portland, Oregon

(2016) R. GORDON QC, R. MOFFATT *Brexit: The Immediate Legal Consequences*, The Constitution Society, London

(2016) D. GRIMM, *Constitutionalism: Past, Present, and Future*, Oxford University

(2019) S. GRUNDMANN, N.V. MICKLITZ (eds.), *The European Banking Union and Constitution: Beacon for Advanced Integration or Death-Knell for Democracy?*, Hart Publishing, London

(1961) A.G. GUEST (ed.), *Oxford Essays in Jurisprudence*, Clarendon Press, Oxford

(2002) C. HARLOW, *Accountability in the European Union*, Oxford University Press

(2014) C. HARLOW, R. RAWLINGS, *Process and Procedure in EU Administration,* Hart Publishing, Oxford and Portland, Oregon

(1979) J.W. HARRIS, *Law and Legal Science. An Inquiry into the Concept of Legal Rule and Legal System*, Clarendon Press, Oxford

(1974) H. HECLO, A. WILDAVSKY, *The Private Government of Public Money: Community and Policy Inside British Politics*, Macmillan, London

(2011) W. HEUN, *The Constitution of Germany: A Contextual Analysis,* Hart Publishing, Oxford and Portland, Oregon

(2019) B. HEUSER, *Brexit in History: Sovereignty or a European Union?*, Hurst & Company, London

(2015) A. HINAREJOS, *The Euro Area Crisis in Constitutional Perspective*, Oxford University Press

(2018) A. HORNE, G. DREWRY (eds.), *Parliament and the Law*, Hart Publishing, Oxford and Portland, Oregon

(2018) A. HORNE, A. LE SUEUR (eds.), *Parliament: Legislation and Accountability*, Hart Publishing, Oxford and Portland, Oregon
(2019) *House of Commons Library. The October 2019 EU – UK Withdrawal Agreement*, 18 October 2019
(2019) D. IBBETSON, N. JONES, N. RAMSAY (eds.), *English Legal History and its Sources: Essay in Honour of Sir John Baker*, Cambridge University Press
(1959) I. JENNINGS, *The Law and the Constitution*, University of London Press, 5th edition, London
(2017) C. JORGES, C. GLINSKI (eds.), *The European Crisis and the Transformation of Transnational Governance*, Hart Publishing, Oxford and Portland, Oregon
(2018) G. KALFLÈCHE, T. PERROUD, M. RUFFERT, *L'Avenir de l'Union économique et monétaire: une perspective franco-allemande*,LGDJ, Lextenso éditions, Issy-les-Moulineaux
(2018) S. KERNEIS (sous la direction de), *Une histoire juridique de l'Occident (III-IXe siècle): Le droit et la coutume* ,Presses Universitaires de France/Humensis, Paris
(2016) M. KING, *The End of Alchemy: Money, Banking and the Future of the Global Economy*, Abacus, London
(1938) H.J. LASKI, *Parliamentary Government in England*, Allen & Unwin, London
(1925) H.J. LASKI, *A Grammar of Politics,* George Allen & Unwin, London
(2009) R. LESAFFER, *European Legal History: A Cultural and Political Perspective*, Cambridge University Press
(1997) P. LEYLAND& T. WOODS (eds.), *Administrative Law Facing the Future: Old Constraints and New Horizons*, Blackstone Press University, London
(2019) A. LYON, *Constitutional History of the UK,* 2nd ed., Routledge, London and New York
(2019) C. MADDOX, *Brexit and Procurement Law*, Routledge, London and New York
(1971) G. MARSHALL, G.C. MOODIE, *Some Problems of the Constitution*, Hutchinson University Library London, 5th ed.
(2018) B. MARTILL, U. STAIGER (eds.), *Brexit and Beyond: Rethinking the Futures of Europe*, UCL Press, London
(2012) A. MINC, *L'âme des nations*, Grasset, Paris
(2019) A. MINC, *Voyage au centre du système*, Grasset, Paris
(2016) N. MOLONEY, *EU Securities and Financial Markets Regulation*, 3rd ed., Oxford University Press
(2017) J. MORPHET, *Beyond Brexit?*, Policy Press University of Bristol, Bristol
(1987) E. MORIN, *Penser l'Europe*, Gallimard, Paris

(2014) D. MÜGGE (ed.), *Europe and the Governance of Global Finance*, Oxford University Press
(2019) E. NANOPOULOS, F. VERGIS (eds.), *The Crisis behind the Eurocrisis*, Cambridge University Press
(2018) K. NICOLAÏDIS, *Exodus, Reckoning, Sacrifice: Three Meanings of Brexit*, Penguin Random House, New York
(2019) K. O'ROURKE, *A Short History of Brexit: From Brentry to Backstop*, Penguin Random UK
(2017) F. PARISI (ed.), *The Oxford Handbook of Law and Economics*, vol. I, Oxford University Press
(2014) J. PEET, A. LAGUARDIA, *Unhappy Union: How the Euro Crisis – and Europe – Can Be Fixed*, Profile Books, London
(2015) K.G. PERSSON, P. SHARP (eds.), *An Economic History of Europe: Knowledge, Institutions and Growth, 600 to the Present*, 2nd ed., Cambridge University Press
(2014) T. PROSSER, *The Economic Constitution*, Oxford University Press
(2017) U. PUETTER, *Brexit and EU Institutional Balance,* Oxford University Press
(1971) J. RAWLS, *A Theory of Justice*, University Press Cambridge, Massachusetts
(2017) M. RYNER, A. CAFRUNY, *The European Union and Global Capitalism: Origins, Development, Crisis*, Palgrave, UK
(2020) V. H. S. E. ROBERTSON, *Competition Law's Innovation Factor: The Relevant Market in Dynamic Context in the EU and the US*, Hart Publishing, Oxford
(1969) H. ROSEVEARE, *The Treasury: the Evolution of a British Institution*, Allen Lane, London
(1973) H.ROSEVEARE, *The Treasury, 1660-1870: The Foundations of Control*, Allen and Unwin
(2011) J. SACHS, *The Price of Civilization: Economics and Ethics After the Fall*, The Bodley Head, London
(1981) P. SALWAY, *Roman Britain: A Very Short Introduction*, Clarendon Press, Oxford
(2015) M. SANDBU, *Europe's Orphan: The Future of the Euro and the Politics of Debt*, Princeton University Press, Princeton and Oxford
(2015) E. SCHMIDT-AßMANN, *The Sources of Administrative Law, Pleading for a More Systematically and Comparative Conception,* AIPDA, Annuario ESI, Napoli
(2015) R. SCHTÜZE, *European Union Law*, Cambridge University Press
(2018) R. SCHÜTZE, S. TIERNEY (eds.), *the United Kingdom and the Federal Idea*, Hart Publishing, Oxford
(1987) A. SEN, *On Ethics & Economics*, Blackwell Publishing, Oxford
(2013) B. SIMMS, *Europe: The Struggle for Supremacy from 1453 to the Present*, Allen Lane, London

(2016) B. SIMMS, *Britain's Europe: A Thousand Years of Conflict and Cooperation*, Penguin Random House, UK

(2016) J.E. STIGLITZ, *The Euro: How a Common Currency Threatens the Future of Europe*, W. W. Norton & Company, New York

(2020) J.E. STIGLITZ, *Rewriting the Rules of the European Economy: An Agenda for Growth and Shared Prosperity*, W. W. Norton & Company, New York

(1997) M. TAGGART (ed.), *The Province of Administrative Law,* Hart Publishing, Oxford

(2017) J. TIROLE, *Economics for the Common Good* (English version), Princeton University Press, Princeton and Oxford

(1976) R.M. UNGER, *Law in Modern Society*, Collier Macmillan Publishers, London

(2019) R.M. UNGER, *The Knowledge Economy*, Verso Publishers, London – New York

(2016) X. VIVES, *Competition and Stability in Banking: The Role of Regulation and Competition Policy*, Princeton University Press, Princeton and Oxford

(2016) S. WEATHERILL, *Law and Values in the European Union*, Clarendon Law Series, Oxford University Press

(2017) S. WEATHERILL, *The Internal Market as a Legal Concept*, Oxford University Press

(2017) P.B. WHYMAN, A.I. PETRESCU, *The Economics of Brexit: A Cost-Benefit Analysis of the UK's Economic Relationship with the EU*, Palgrave Macmillan, London

B) Documents

The below listed documents are exclusively those from which quotations are reported in the text book. The fonts in boldface are the abbreviations used in the text.

UK Government, 31.12.2020, **EU (Future Relationship) Act,** *The European Union (Future Relationship) Act 2020 (Commencement No. 1) Regulations 2020*,
https://www.legislation.gov.uk/uksi/2020/1662/made/data.pdf

EU COM, 26.12.2020, **Joint Declaration,** *Joint Declaration on Financial Services Regulatory Cooperation between the European Union and the United Kingdom*,
https://eur-lex.europa.eu/legal-content/EN/TXT/PDF/?uri=CELEX:22020A1231(03)&from=EN

EU COM, 26.12.2020, **The EU-UK Civil Nuclear Agreement**, *Agreement between the Government of the United Kingdom of Great Britain and Northern Ireland and the European Atomic Energy Community for Cooperation on the safe and peaceful uses of nuclear energy*, https://eur-lex.europa.eu/legal-content/EN/TXT/PDF/?uri=CELEX:22020A1231(04)&from=EN

EU COM, 25.12.2020, **Explanatory Memorandum,** *annex to the Proposal for a Council Decision on the conclusion on behalf of the Union, of the Trade and Cooperation Agreement between the European Union and the European Atomic Energy Community, of the one partCOM (2020) 856 final*, https://ec.europa.eu/info/sites/info/files/brexit_files/info_site/com_2020_856_act_en.pdf

EU COM, 24.12.2020, **EU-UK Trade and Cooperation Agreement,** *Trade and Cooperation Agreeement between the European Union and the European Atomic Energy Community, of the one part, and the United Kingdom of Great Britain and Northern Ireland, of the other part*, https://ec.europa.eu/info/sites/info/files/brexit_files/info_site/tca-20-12-28.pdf

UK Government TCA Summary, 24.12.2020, H.M Government, *UK-EU Trade and Cooperation Agreement*, https://assets.publishing.service.gov.uk/government/uploads/system/uploads/attachment_data/file/948093/TCA_SUMMARY_PDF.pd

European Parliament, 17.12.2020, **EU Recovery Instrument and the Rule of Law Regulation**, *European Parliament resolution of 17 December 2020 on the Multiannual Financial Framework 2021-2027, the Interistitutional Agreement, the EU Recovery Instrument and the Rule of Law Regulation (2020/2923 (RSP)*, https://www.europarl.europa.eu/doceo/document/TA-9-2020-0360_EN.pdf

UK Internal Market Act, 17.12.2020, **UK Parliament,** *United Kingdom Internal Market Act 2020*, https://www.legislation.gov.uk/ukpga/2020/27/enacted/data.pdf

EU COM, 13.10.2020, **Temporary Framework Amendment,** Communication from the Commission, - *4th Amendment to the Temporary Framework for State aid measures to support the economy in the current COVID-19 outbreak and amendment to the Annex to the Communication from the Commission to the Member States on the application of Articles 107 and 108 of the Treaty on the Functioning of the European Union to short-term export-credit insurance,* C(2020) 7127 final, https://ec.europa.eu/competition/state_aid/what_is_new/sa_covid19_4th_amendment_and_prolongation_temporary_framework_en.pdf

EU COM, 1.10.2020, **EU Letter,** *Withdrawal Agreement: European Commission sends letter of formal notice to the United Kingdom for breach of its obligations*, https://ec.europa.eu/commission/presscorner/detail/en/ip_20_1798

EU COM, 17.9.2020, **NGEU Guidelines,** *Commission Staff Working Document, Guidance To Member States, Recovery and Resilience Plans*, SWD(2020) 205 final, https://ec.europa.eu/info/sites/info/files/3_en_document_travail_service_part1_v3_en_0.pdf

UK Internal Market White Paper, July 2020, *Department for Business, Energy & Industrial Strategy, UK Internal Market*, https://www.gov.uk/government/publications/uk-internal-market

EU COM, 9.7.2020, **EU Policy Paper 2020,** Communication from the Commission, – *Communication on readiness at the end of the transition period between the European Union and the United Kingdom*, COM (2020) 324 final, https://ec.europa.eu/info/sites/info/files/brexit_files/info_site/com_2020_324_2_communication_from_commission_to_inst_en_0.pdf

EU COM, 2.7.2020, **Temporary Framework Amendment,** Communication from Commission, - *Third Amendment to the Temporary Framework for State aid measures to support the economy in the current COVID-19 outbreak,* (2020/C218/03), https://eur-lex.europa.eu/legal-content/EN/TXT/PDF/?uri=CELEX:52020XC0702(01)&from=EN

EU COM, 8.5.2020, **Temporary Framework Amendment,** Communication from the Commission, – *Amendment to the Temporary Framework for State aid measures to support the economy in the current COVID-19 outbreak,* C (2020) 3156 final, https://ec.europa.eu/competition/state_aid/what_is_new/sa_covid19_2nd_amendment_temporary_framework_en.pdf

EU Council, 9.4.2020 **Report,** *Report on the comprehensive economic policy response to the COVID-19 pandemic*, https://www.consilium.europa.eu/it/press/press-releases/2020/04/09/report-on-the-comprehensive-economic-policy-response-to-the-covid-19-pandemic/

EU COM, 3.4.2020, **Temporary Framework Amendment,** Communication from the Commission, – *Amendment to the Temporary Framework for State aid measures to support the economy in the current COVID-19 outbreak*, C (2020) 2215 final, https://ec.europa.eu/competition/state_aid/what_is_new/sa_covid19_1st_amendment_temporary_framework_en.pdf

EU COM, 20.3.2020, **EU Communication,** *Communication from the Commission to the Council on the activation of the general escape clause of the Stability and Growth Pact*, COM (2020) 123 final, https://ec.europa.eu/info/sites/info/files/economy-finance/2_en_act_part1_v3-adopted_text.pdf

EU COM, 19.3.2020, **Temporary Framework,** Communication from the Commission, – *Temporary Framework for State aid measures to support the economy in the current COVID-19 outbreak*, C (2020) 1863 final, https://ec.europa.eu/competition/state_aid/what_is_new/sa_covid19_temporary-framework.pdf

EU Draft Text, 18.3.2020, European Commission, Task Force for Relations with the United Kingdom, *Draft text of the Agreement on the New Partnership with the United Kingdom*, https://ec.europa.eu/info/sites/info/files/200318-draft-agreement-gen.pdf

UK's Approach to negotiations, 27.2.2020, H.M. Government, *The Future Relationship with the EU – The UK's Approach to Negotiations*, https://assets.publishing.service.gov.uk/government/uploads/system/uploads/attachment_data/file/868874/The_Future_Relationship_with_the_EU.pdf

Directives for negotiation 25.2.2020, Council of the European Union, *Directives for the negotiation of a new partnership with the United Kingdom of Great Britain and Northern Ireland*, https://www.consilium.europa.eu/media/42736/st05870-ad01re03-en20.pdf

European Commission Recommendation, 3.2.2020, – European Commission Recommendation for a Council Decision *authorising the opening of negotiations for a new partnership with the United Kingdom of Great Britain and Northern Ireland*, COM (2020) 35 final, https://eur-lex.europa.eu/resource.html?uri=cellar:03e2bee1-4679-11ea-b81b-01aa75ed71a1.0016.02/DOC_1&format=PDF

European Recommendation, 23.1.2020, – *European Parliament Recommendation on the draft Council decision on the conclusion of the Agreement on the withdrawal of the United Kingdom of Great Britain and Northern Ireland from the European Union and the European Atomic Energy Community,* A9-0004/2020, https://www.europarl.europa.eu/doceo/document/A-9-2020-0004_EN.pdf

EUWA, 23.1.2020, – *European Union (Withdrawal Agreement) Act 2018*, amended as *European Union (Withdrawal Agreement) Act 2020*, http://www.legislation.gov.uk/ukpga/2020/1

Withdrawal Agreement, 12.11.2019, Council, *Agreement on the withdrawal of the United Kingdom of Great Britain and Northern Ireland from the European Union and the European Atomic Energy Community* (2019/C 384 I/01), https://eur-lex.europa.eu/legal-content/EN/TXT/PDF/?uri=CELEX:12019W/TXT(02)&from=EN

Political Declaration, 19.10.2019, *Political Declaration on setting out the framework for the future relationship between the European Union and the United Kingdom*, https://assets.publishing.service.gov.uk/government/uploads/system/uploads/attachment_data/file/840656/Political_Declaration_setting_out_the_framework_for_the_future_relationship_between_the_European_Union_and_the_United_Kingdom.pdf

Franco-German Manifesto, 20.2.2019, Bundesministerium für Wirtschaft und Energie, *A Franco-German Manifesto for a European industrial policy fit for the 2st Century*, https://www.bmwi.de/Redaktion/DE/Downloads/F/franco-german-manifesto-for-a-european-industrial-policy.pdf%3F__blob%3DpublicationFile%26v%3D2

Legal Position, December 2018, H.M. Government, Attorney General, *EU Exit Legal position on the Withdrawal Agreement*, December 2018, https://assets.publishing.service.gov.uk/government/uploads/system/uploads/

attachment_data/file/761153/EU_Exit_-_Legal_position_on_the_Witdrawal_Agreement.pdf

White Paper (November 2018), H.M. Government, *EU Exit Taking back control of our borders, money and laws while protecting our economy, security and Union*, https://assets.publishing.service.gov.uk/government/uploads/system/uploads/attachment_data/file/759792/28_November_EU_Exit_-_Taking_back_control_of_our_borders__money_and_laws_while_protecting_our_economy__security_and_Union__1_.pdf

White Paper (July 2018), H.M. Government, *The future relationship between the United Kingdom and the European Union*, https://assets.publishing.service.gov.uk/government/uploads/system/uploads/attachment_data/file/786626/The_Future_Relationship_between_the_United_Kingdom_and_the_European_Union_120319.pdf

White Paper (2017) H.M. Government, *The United Kingdom's exit from and new partnership with the European Union,* February 2017, updated in May 2017, https://assets.publishing.service.gov.uk/government/uploads/system/uploads/attachment_data/file/786626/The_Future_Relationship_between_the_United_Kingdom_and_the_European_Union_120319.pdf

White Paper (2016) H.M. Government, *The process for withdrawing from the European Union*, February 2016, https://assets.publishing.service.gov.uk/government/uploads/system/uploads/attachment_data/file/503908/54538_EU_Series_No2_Accessible.pdf

Settlement, 18-19.2.2016 – European Council *Decision of the Heads of State or Government, meeting within the European Council, concerning a new Settlement for the United Kingdom within the European Union*, https://www.consilium.europa.eu/media/21787/0216-euco-conclusions.pdf

INDEX

For Product Safety Concerns and Information please contact our EU
representative GPSR@taylorandfrancis.com
Taylor & Francis Verlag GmbH, Kaufingerstraße 24, 80331 München, Germany

www.ingramcontent.com/pod-product-compliance
Ingram Content Group UK Ltd.
Pitfield, Milton Keynes, MK11 3LW, UK
UKHW022129190926
475702UK00013B/1715

* 9 7 8 1 0 3 2 0 5 5 4 0 4 *